HEALTH PSYCHOLOGY RESEARCH FOCUS

SEXUAL ABUSE

INTERVENTION, COPING STRATEGIES AND PSYCHOLOGICAL IMPACT

HEALTH PSYCHOLOGY RESEARCH FOCUS

Additional books in this series can be found on Nova's website under the Series tab.

Additional e-books in this series can be found on Nova's website under the e-book tab.

SEXUAL ABUSE

INTERVENTION, COPING STRATEGIES AND PSYCHOLOGICAL IMPACT

OLIVIA PARSONS
EDITOR

nova
publishers
New York

NOTICE TO THE READER

Library of Congress Cataloging-in-Publication Data

ISBN: 978-1-63484-509-0

Published by Nova Science Publishers, Inc. † *New York*

CONTENTS

Preface   vii

Chapter 1   A Group Intervention for Nonoffending Parents
                 and Caregivers of Child Victims of Sexual Abuse
                 Jennifer M. Foster   1

Chapter 2   Child Sexual Abuse: Awareness, Sensitization
                 and Therapeutic Intervention for School Children:
                 Indian Scenario   25
                 P. B. Behere, A. N. Mulmule, A. P. Behere,
                 R. Yadav and A. A. Sinha

Chapter 3   Cultural Competence and Child Interviewing:
                 Understanding Religious Factors in Child Sexual
                 Abuse Interviewing   45
                 Karen L. Haboush, Anne Meltzer,
                 Rachel Wang and Narmene Hamsho

Chapter 4   Sexual Abuse and the Psychological Impact
                 on Children: A Review of the Literature   89
                 Allison N. Sinanan

Chapter 5   Invisible Victims: A Review of the Literature
                 on Male Sexual Abuse   101
                 Jennifer M. Foster

Index   129

PREFACE

Approximately 1 in 4 girls and 1 in 6 boys below the age of 18 are victims of child sexual abuse (CSA) according to the Centers for Disease Control and Prevention. A wealth of peer-reviewed literature has investigated interventions for child victims and adult survivors of CSA; however, there has been a lack of focus on the therapeutic needs of nonoffending parents and caregivers (NOPC) of child victims. In the wake of their children's sexual abuse, NOPC are at risk of a host of mental health disorders, and researchers estimate their symptomology continues for two years following the disclosure or discovery. *Sexual Abuse: Intervention, Coping Strategies and Psychological Impact* begins with a framework for group counseling for NOPC, and discusses alternative and parallel interventions for NOPC while providing recommendations for future research. Chapter Two continues on to provides an overview of CSA and intervention in India. Chapter Three focuses on two historically persecuted groups, Orthodox Jews and Muslims, and the religious values that may enhance culturally competent interviewing skills in child sexual abuse interviews. Chapter Four presents potential cognitive mediators associated with the psychological impact of childhood sexual abuse by reviewing past and current literature on the effects of this type of abuse. Chapter Five addresses the gap in current knowledge and understanding of male sexual abuse.

Chapter 1 – Approximately 1 in 4 girls and 1 in 6 boys below the age of 18 are victims of child sexual abuse (CSA) according to the Centers for Disease Control and Prevention (2005). A wealth of peer-reviewed literature has investigated interventions for child victims and adult survivors of CSA; however, there has been a lack of focus on the therapeutic needs of nonoffending parents and caregivers (NOPC) of child victims (Tavkar &

Hansen, 2011). In the wake of their children's sexual abuse, NOPC are at risk of a host of mental health disorders, and researchers estimate their symptomology continues for two years following the disclosure or discovery (Stauffer & Deblinger, 1996). Although the risk of negative outcomes is high for NOPC, counseling services can effectively reduce symptoms for adults (Grosz, Kempe, & Kelly, 1999) and simultaneously improve outcomes for child victims (Cohen & Mannarino, 2000; Corcoran, 2004; Deblinger, Stauffer, & Steer, 2001; Feather & Ronan, 2009; Heflin, Deblinger, & Fisher, 2000; Silverman et al., 2008). This chapter provides a framework for group counseling for NOPC, including: (a) the unique needs of NOPC, (b) group components, (c) curriculum, and (d) special considerations. This chapter concludes with alternative and parallel interventions for NOPC and provides recommendations for future research.

Chapter 2 – Nearly 19% of the world's child population, lives in India and children form 42% of the total Indian population. Child Sexual abuse (CSA) in India is an under reported offence but has acquired the nature of an epidemic. Studies across the country have reported a staggering statistic, of every second child being the victim of some or the other form of sexual abuse. Moreover, every fifth child has been reported to have experienced severe forms of sexual abuse. Results of the famous study, the 'Study on Child Abuse India 2007', acted as an eye opener. This suggests the need to increase the awareness regarding CSA and sensitize the prime persons in a child's life viz. parents, teachers and peers, who can bring a definite change in the intervention by reporting it early. Girls are more prone than boys and school going children (7 -13 years) form the most vulnerable age group. There are many unreported and un-noticed cases. On the notion *"axe soon forgets but the tree remembers,"* CSA is considered to be a universal problem with lifelong significant impact nearly in all aspects of life. All CSA victims need therapy and early intervention to prevent later symptomatology. Children tend to face psychological, behavioral and social difficulties. Thus, early intervention is encouraged and is based on notion of *protect, suspect, inspect, collect* and *respect*. The type of therapy to be provided is divided into psychotherapy, creative therapies (including Dynamic play therapy, art therapy or drama therapy), Eye Movement Desensitization & Reprocessing (EMDR). In India, self-help groups of victims & families are another good approach. Several preventive measures established are help lines, awareness programs and community support systems. India has brought several reforms in the existing Indian laws to safe- guard the interest of victims. The most recent of the amendments is the "Criminal Law Act 2013." Finally, the reality lies in the fact that 'everyone can and should report' suspected sexual abuse. Thus considering the magnitude of the problem, this is an effort to provide an overview of Child Sexual Abuse and intervention in the Indian scenario.

Chapter 3 – Increasingly, the literature on child sexual abuse recognizes the importance of considering cultural factors, including ethnicity and religion, when interviewing and intervening with children. While interviewing children about alleged sexual abuse is always challenging, there is growing acknowledgement of the unique challenges associated with interviewing members of orthodox religious communities. Religious values, including views of sexuality, family structure, and collectivist versus individual norms, may all influence children's reporting. In particular, concerns about the potential for alienating oneself or one's family from the larger religious community may hinder reporting of child sexual abuse. Experiences of religious discrimination and persecution may further contribute to the desire to protect one's religious community from added shame. For these reasons, school personnel, who are mandated reporters, may encounter opposition to their decision to report, despite the increasingly diverse population of public school students, as well as the increase in faith-based schools. Although research within religious communities on child sexual abuse is limited, a growing clinical literature is emerging. This chapter will focus on two historically persecuted groups, Orthodox Jews and Muslims, and the religious values that may enhance culturally competent interviewing skills. Cultural sensitivity requires knowledge and skill in aligning child interviewing techniques with religious values and incorporating community resources: components of forensic interviewing and case examples will be discussed to illustrate these concepts.

Chapter 4 – Research to date has indicated that the psychological effects of childhood sexual abuse are multiple, extensive, and characterized by a boundless amount of variability. Various factors such as frequency and duration of abuse, type of sexual contact, the degree of relationship between the perpetrator and victim will result in differential psychological effects. Experts differ regarding the psychological impact of child sexual abuse, with opinions ranging from the widely-held belief that the impact is vast and irreversible to the controversial perspective that it has very little psychological impact on the child (Gagnon, 1965; La Barbera, Martin, & Dozier, 1980; Mannarino & Cohen, 1986). Many of the early studies reporting minimal impact from child sexual abuse relied more upon anecdotal evidence, calling into question the reliability of their findings. Other studies have been retrospective. Victims of child sexual abuse present with a diverse variety of symptoms rather than a specific abuse profile, and symptom levels for sexually abused children. This chapter will present potential cognitive mediators associated with the psychological impact of childhood sexual abuse by reviewing past and current literature on the effects of this type of abuse.

Chapter 5 – Child sexual abuse (CSA) is a pervasive global problem (Johnson, 2004). Although boys frequently experience sexual abuse, a disparate amount of attention has been given to male victims in the empirical literature. The vast majority of research on CSA includes predominately adult females and their recollections of CSA (Sorsoli, Kia-Keating & Grossman, 2008; Wilhite, 2015). Research samples with only females or with few men represented are extremely limited in their generalizability. Although there are numerous similarities between male and female victims, recent research has uncovered several distinct differences (Hopton & Huta, 2013). This review of the literature addresses the gap in current knowledge and understanding of male sexual abuse by exploring: (a) the prevalence of male sexual abuse, (b) victim and perpetrator characteristics, (c) disclosure, (d) short- and long-term outcomes for male survivors, (e) treatment, and (f) the healing journey.

In: Sexual Abuse
Editor: Olivia Parsons

ISBN: 978-1-63484-509-0
© 2016 Nova Science Publishers, Inc.

Chapter 1

A GROUP INTERVENTION FOR NONOFFENDING PARENTS AND CAREGIVERS OF CHILD VICTIMS OF SEXUAL ABUSE

Jennifer M. Foster[*]
Department of Counselor Education and Counseling Psychology,
Western Michigan University, MI, US

ABSTRACT

Approximately 1 in 4 girls and 1 in 6 boys below the age of 18 are victims of child sexual abuse (CSA) according to the Centers for Disease Control and Prevention (2005). A wealth of peer-reviewed literature has investigated interventions for child victims and adult survivors of CSA; however, there has been a lack of focus on the therapeutic needs of nonoffending parents and caregivers (NOPC) of child victims (Tavkar & Hansen, 2011). In the wake of their children's sexual abuse, NOPC are at risk of a host of mental health disorders, and researchers estimate their symptomology continues for two years following the disclosure or discovery (Stauffer & Deblinger, 1996). Although the risk of negative outcomes is high for NOPC, counseling services can effectively reduce symptoms for adults (Grosz, Kempe, & Kelly, 1999) and simultaneously improve outcomes for child victims (Cohen & Mannarino, 2000;

[*] Correspondence concerning this article should be addressed to Jennifer M. Foster, Department of Counselor Education and Counseling Psychology, Western Michigan University, 3102 Sangren Hall, Kalamazoo, MI 49008 USA (email: Jennifer.Foster@wmich.edu).

Corcoran, 2004; Deblinger, Stauffer, & Steer, 2001; Feather & Ronan, 2009; Heflin, Deblinger, & Fisher, 2000; Silverman et al., 2008). This chapter provides a framework for group counseling for NOPC, including: (a) the unique needs of NOPC, (b) group components, (c) curriculum, and (d) special considerations. This chapter concludes with alternative and parallel interventions for NOPC and provides recommendations for future research.

INTRODUCTION

Child sexual abuse (CSA) is a pervasive, global problem that is estimated to impact 1 in 4 girls and 1 in 6 boys before the age of 18 (Centers for Disease Control and Prevention, 2005). CSA also effects non-offending parents and caregivers (hereafter referred to as NOPC). Research indicates that most children are sexually abused by someone they (and their families) know and trust. Offenders include adults as well as older or more dominant children. Approximately 40% of sexually abusive acts are committed by perpetrators who are under the age of 18 (Finkelhor, 2012). Although stranger initiated sexual abuse or assault occurs, it only accounts for 3-10% of cases, with adolescents being most at risk for this type of victimization (Finkelhor, Hammer, & Sedlak, 2008).

There are a host of short- and long-term ramifications for child victims of sexual abuse (Goldfinch, 2009; Tomlinson, 2008). When counseling interventions are employed following the disclosure, treatment is often successful in the reduction of trauma-related symptoms (Green, 2008). Many children return to their pre-trauma level of functioning and demonstrate posttraumatic growth (Leckman & Mayes, 2007).

Unfortunately, some challenges continue into adulthood. This is especially true for those who did not have an opportunity as children to process their trauma in the safety of a therapeutic relationship. Some of the most common negative outcomes are: mental health diagnoses (e.g., depression, anxiety, posttraumatic stress), relational challenges (e.g., sexual health, intimacy, and increased risk for sexual assault and domestic violence), and spiritual concerns (e.g., changed belief system).

Recent strides have been made to raise awareness about sexual abuse. Media coverage has brought attention to cases of CSA with the majority of news stories focusing on trusted community members such as teachers, coaches, and religious leaders (Green, 2008). Despite this increased attention, there are still many misconceptions about CSA that protect offenders and hinder victims and their families. For example, familial sexual abuse, which includes sibling sexual abuse is rarely discussed publicly. Further, sibling sexual abuse may be the most common type of sexual abuse in families (Welfare, 2008), and it frequently involves the use of force and penetration (Tremblay, Hebert, & Piche, 1999). Although common, abuse within the family is often perceived as a shameful, taboo subject, and NOPC experience additional self-blame for not seeing the warning signs.

Sexual abuse is difficult for NOPC to address due to its frequent occurrence in the context of relationships that are built on trust. Friends and family of the victim may react in disbelief and side with the offender, who many view as beyond reproach (van Dam, 2006). NOPC may be tempted to not report CSA because of the belief that it will be worse for their child if the abuse is made public. The reaction of most NOPC is to protect their child from further abuse, but they do not realize that by not reporting the abuse, they are giving the perpetrator an opportunity to continue to offend others.

Unfortunately, some NOPC respond to their child's disclosure with disbelief. The failure to believe their child and maintain status quo places their children at high risk for additional abuse. This is a frightening and confusing experience for children (Oz, 2005).

Conversely, there are NOPC who believe their children and report the abuse immediately. Their children are more likely to experience positive outcomes despite the trauma they have experienced. Multiple studies have demonstrated a correlation between parental support following disclosure and the child's subsequent mental health (for a review see Elliott & Carnes, 2001). Further, adult survivors of sexual abuse are less likely to experience mental health problems if their mother was supportive following their childhood disclosure (Easton, 2012).

Even with NOPC support and belief, the family is in a state of crisis following abuse discovery or disclosure (Oz, 2005). "CSA affects the family system. It can change marital relationships, parenting styles, relationships between the victim and siblings, grandparents, aunts and uncles as the meaning of sex and touch has been changed" (Jones & Morris, 2007, p. 225). Knowledge of their child's sexual abuse is traumatizing for NOPC and results in a host of feelings such as self-blame, anger, and sadness. One of the most common feelings is guilt for not being able to protect their child.

The situation is further complicated for NOPC when the offender was known. The relationship is severed (by a protective parent), and a domino effect of consequences ensues. NOPC may be required to relocate if they lived with or near the perpetrator. If the perpetrator was a spouse or paramour, the

NOPC must initiate divorce or separation. Although this is a protective response, it typically has financial repercussions. NOPC also face loss of support when friends or family side with the perpetrator. Further, involvement in the legal system is an additional stressor for child victims and NOPC. Moreover, NOPC with a personal history of CSA are even more likely to experience significant distress (Hiebert-Murphy, 1998).

In the wake of this devastating experience, families need support from a counselor (Corcoran, 2004, Foster, 2014). Unfortunately, there has been a lack of focus on the therapeutic needs of NOPC (Tavkar & Hansen, 2011). Research has established that NOPC are at risk for a host of mental health disorders, and their symptomology continues for two years following the abuse disclosure or discovery (Stauffer & Deblinger, 1996).

Although the risk of negative outcomes is high for NOPC, counseling services can effectively reduce symptoms for adults (Grosz et al., 1999) and simultaneously improve outcomes for child victims (Cohen & Mannarino, 2000; Corcoran, 2004; Deblinger et al., 2001; Feather & Ronan, 2009; Heflin et al., 2000; Silverman et al., 2008). This chapter provides a framework for group counseling for NOPC of child victims of sexual abuse, including: (a) the unique needs of NOPC, (b) group components, (c) curriculum, and (d) special considerations. This chapter concludes with alternative and parallel interventions for NOPC, and suggestions for future research are provided.

GROUP COUNSELING TO ADDRESS THE UNIQUE NEEDS OF NOPC

Following the life altering discovery that one's child has been abused, NOPC experience numerous personal reactions, relational changes, financial ramifications, and transitions that impact one's feeling of stability and security. This is an overwhelming time for NOPC, and their need for support is high. The group format provides an outlet for NOPC to express their thoughts and feelings about their children's abuse. In this setting, they can ask questions, receive feedback, and create a plan for healing and moving forward. The following section details the unique needs of NOPC who are "secondary victims" (McCourt, Peel, & O'Carroll, 1998) of the crime their children experienced.

Personal Reactions

For NOPC, personal reactions often include shock/denial, anger, sadness, blame, guilt, and embarrassment. Disbelief is a common initial reaction. It does not seem possible that this could happen to their child. It also does not seem possible, when the offender is known and trusted, that he/she is capable of the abuse. NOPC in this stage may try to come up with an explanation for the offender's behaviors. They may try to convince themselves that their child was confused or misperceived what was happening. NOPC who are unable to move past shock or denial, dismiss perpetrators' actions and attempt to move forward without proper reporting of the abuse or obtaining help for the child victim. This has devastating consequences for children (Oz, 2005).

Anger is another common reaction for NOPC. For some, anger quickly follows the initial shock. Many children in their narratives about sexual abuse described their NOPC expressing anger following a disclosure (Foster & Hagedorn, 2014a). Children described their NOPC yelling at them or at the offender if they were present. Anger for some NOPC lasts a long time. For example, one father in a group session described his anger building up inside him to the point he went outside and burned down the treehouse where the perpetrator had abused his daughter. Group counselors provide opportunities for clients to safely express their anger during group through therapeutic interventions.

Beneath anger is often a deep sadness experienced by NOPC. It is a sadness for what has been lost: their child's innocence, life as they knew it, and the possibility of a relationship with the offender. It can also result in a loss of believing that the world is a safe place and that most people are good. Symptoms of sadness sometimes evolve into depression, which can reach clinical levels and require additional treatments (individual counseling and/or medication). Group counselors working with NOPC must monitor group members for symptoms of depression and provide additional supports when needed.

Along with sadness, many NOPC report feeling embarrassed or ashamed that CSA happened in their family. They may desire to keep it a secret from friends, coworkers, and even family members. Carrying this secret comes at a price for both the NOPC and child victim, who may be internalizing the shame. Group counselors can help NOPC explore their hesitancy to tell others about the abuse and explore if it comes from a place of protection for their child or if it is causing their child further distress.

In addition to embarrassment, most NOPC experience a combination of guilt and blame, which can be explored and processed in the group context. Blame can be directed at oneself or others, including: the perpetrator, other adults, or even the child victim. Self-blame is very common. NOPC, especially those who knew the perpetrator, wonder how they missed the warning signs of abuse. They also wonder how they could have been so deceived by the offender. They replay scene after scene in their mind, looking for clues. Sometimes when NOPC learn about the warning signs, they realize offenders' behaviors or children's abuse symptoms that they missed or dismissed. This can lead to feelings of personal guilt and self-blame that need to be explored in a supportive group atmosphere.

NOPC may also blame other adults responsible for supervision of the child victim, such as a teacher if the abuse happened at school by another adult or child. Another example is blaming the church or youth organization where the abuse occurred. NOPC leave their children in the care of others expecting proper supervision and organizational policies to be upheld, but this does not always happen. Poor screening processes, failure to hold all workers/volunteers to standards, or treating certain people as if they are above reproach allows for sexual abuse to occur in such settings. Group leaders can help NOPC process their thoughts and feelings about those who failed to protect their children.

It is also important for group leaders to be aware that some NOPC blame the child victim. In an attempt to understand what happened, they may hold their child responsible for not stopping the abuse or telling sooner. Group leaders can help NOPC understand the manipulation used by perpetrators to prevent children from ending the abuse or disclosing. Children do not always recognize that the act was abusive, especially if it did not cause pain. Children may experience confusion, but may not be able to put into words that something is wrong. Further, children are taught by NOPC to respect adults (or older children in a caregiving role) and do what they say without question. The group setting allows for NOPC to be honest about their feelings of blame toward the child and move to a place of viewing the offender as fully responsible.

Blame directed at the perpetrator must also be processed in group. This is the person responsible for the pain caused to their child and them. Unfortunately, many NOPC will not see the offender convicted of the abuse. It is difficult to capture conviction rates for crimes against children. With adults, only 14-18% of reported sexual assaults lead to prosecution (Patterson & Campbell, 2010), and the conviction rate of these reported crimes is only 18%

(Tjaden & Thoennes, 2006). Having charges dropped or a "not guilty" verdict can cause NOPC to cycle back to anger, sadness, or blame. Group leaders can process these and other personal reactions that NOPC experience in the wake of sexual abuse. It is also necessary to explore relational changes as a result of the sexual abuse, which are discussed in the next section.

Relational Changes

Following CSA, NOPC experience numerous changes in relationships. This adds to their feelings of aloneness and instability. Relational changes include coping with the loss of a relationship with the perpetrator (when known by the NOPC), dealing with disbelief, denial, or lack of support from relatives, friends, and the community, a changed relationship with the child victim, and the potential for a changed relationship with God or a higher power.

Given that most sexual offenders are known and trusted by NOPC, the result is a severance of the relationship with the offender (when the child is believed). This is often sudden and leaves the NOPC with many questions. The situation is complicated when the perpetrator is a spouse, paramour, or other close family member. The betrayal that is experienced is tremendous not only for the child victim but also for the NOPC. If the NOPC was in a position of dependence on the offender, this can lead to financial ramifications and instability which are discussed in subsequent sections.

The support and belief of their child does not always result in others believing the child and supporting the family. When CSA occurs in the context of a family, it often causes members to declare allegiance to either the perpetrator or victim. This is especially hurtful for victims and NOPC who desperately need the support of others. The group can be a pseudo family during this time of crisis by providing a caring, supportive network.

Beyond the immediate family, others may also question whether or not the offender really harmed the victim. When friends, coworkers, or community members question the victim's account instead of the perpetrator's story, NOPC often feel isolated. For example, one former group member shared that her husband was a leader in their church and community. Even after a forensic exam revealed physical evidence that he had assaulted her daughter, church members stood behind him and continued to visit him in prison after he was convicted.

Another common consequence following disclosure or discovery of CSA is a changed relationship between the NOPC and child victim. The child may regret disclosing or feel blamed by the NOPC based on how they reacted to the disclosure. NOPC may view their child differently post-abuse, and worry about the short- and long-term ramifications. Many children may still care for their perpetrator, which can be difficult for NOPC to understand. Although the abuse was disclosed, children may feel that the topic cannot be talked about further. They may avoid it out of fear of angering or causing sadness to their NOPC. An important role of group counselors is to help NOPC reconnect with their children, communicate belief, and provide opportunities to talk about the abuse and subsequent events openly.

A final NOPC relationship that may change depending on their beliefs is with God (or a higher power). NOPC may view God differently after CSA. They may have questions about God, such as his goodness or power to stop evil. They may question God's care for them and provision. While some NOPC may turn towards God, others may turn away or experience changed beliefs. This can be complicated when abuse occurs in the context of a religious setting and at the hands of "religious" people.

In sum, a child's disclosure is the beginning of numerous relational changes for NOPC and their family. Group counselors can provide an opportunity for NOPC to express their thoughts and feelings about these changes. Further, counselors can help NOPC identify ways to strengthen their relationships with their children and receive support from group members.

Financial Challenges

As a consequence of changed relationships, many NOPC experience financial changes. When the offender is a spouse, partner, or paramour, the decision to leave or divorce the individual likely results in an income loss. Suddenly being a single parent is overwhelming, especially if the NOPC had been out of the work force or underemployed. The NOPC may experience difficulty meeting the basic needs of their family, which could lead to a need for government support. Navigating the system to attain this support can be confusing and frustrating. In addition to basic living expenses, some families must also pay legal fees related to the prosecution of the offender. It may take some time for families to regain financial stability. Group counselors can connect NOPC with community advocates and caseworkers who can provide help with basic needs (e.g., food, clothing, utility bills, and transportation) and legal costs during this time of crisis.

Transitional Experiences

There are numerous transitions for NOPC and their families in the wake of CSA. Many of these cause feelings of instability. For example, relocation is a common occurrence. If the family resided with the perpetrator and the perpetrator was not charged with a crime following investigation, the NOPC may be forced to move. Additionally, the NOPC may wish to relocate to a different neighborhood, school, daycare center, or place of worship if the perpetrator is not convicted. Even if the perpetrator experiences legal consequences, unsupportive or unbelieving others may make returning to these places excruciating for the NOPC and child victim. Groups can provide support for NOPC during these transitions.

In sum, group counseling is a modality that is able to address the unique needs faced by NOPC. Many NOPC experience significant distress and isolation due to their personal, relational, financial, and transitional experiences. Group members have the opportunity to process their reactions to the abuse and feelings about the perpetrator, their child, and themselves. Additionally, they can receive support, share resources, decrease their feelings of isolation, and regain a sense of stability. One of the most powerful experiences in NOPC groups is that of universality, which is defined as group members realizing they are not alone in the problems they are facing. Universality is one of the factors that leads to therapeutic change and healing in group therapy (Yalom & Leszcz, 2005). The following section discusses components of a successful group that facilitates healing for NOPC and their families.

GROUP COMPONENTS

There are several components that increase the likelihood of a successful group for NOPC. They are effective leaders, an open group format, and attention to group dynamics. Each of these is discussed below.

Effective Leadership

Effective group leaders are essential to the success of the group for NOPC. Qualities of an effective group leader include: courage, willingness to model, presence, goodwill, genuineness, and caring, belief in group process, openness, non-defensiveness in coping with criticism, becoming aware of your own culture, willingness to seek new experiences, personal power, stamina, self-awareness, sense of humor, inventiveness, and personal dedication and commitment (Corey & Corey, 2006). In addition, group leaders of NOPC must have training in the area of sexual abuse as well as experience facilitating groups. Group leaders must understand the healing process for families impacted by CSA. They must also be able to provide referrals to meet members' needs (e.g., caseworkers, advocates, social workers).

Open Format

Groups for NOPC benefit from an open group format, which is "characterized by changing membership" (Corey & Corey, 2006, p. 118). For the NOPC group, it is ideal to meet consistently (typically on a weekly basis for 90-120 minutes) on the same day and time throughout the year. This allows for ongoing enrollment, which results in fast access to services following the disclosure of CSA. Members should commit to a minimum number of sessions (e.g., six sessions) to provide additional stability to the group. Additionally, if a member misses more than two sessions without contact or a valid reason, they will not be allowed to continue to attend (Corey & Corey).

One of the most important aspects of the open group format is that the more senior members can provide support and encouragement to new members. Senior members may not be aware of their progress until they help someone who is at a different stage of healing. New members have the benefit of others who understand what they are going through. Members come alongside each other as they navigate life post-abuse.

Group Dynamics

In addition to implementing an open group format, leaders must attend to group dynamics to increase the likelihood of positive group outcomes for members. Specifically, leaders must consider group referrals, screening procedures, group size, and composition.

To form an initial group, leaders must advertise the group in their agency as well as the community. Referrals from other practitioners are also helpful to identify NOPC who would benefit from this group.

Each member should be screened for appropriateness for the group setting. To qualify, they must be a NOPC of a child victim of sexual abuse. The abuse must have been reported and their child must be receiving treatment either individually or in a group. Additionally, the group leader should ask the NOPC about personal history of sexual abuse and assess whether or not this has been addressed. If the NOPC has an unprocessed history of CSA, individual counseling is generally recommended prior to beginning group membership. Further, the group leader should recommend individual counseling for those who are experiencing clinically significant symptom distress. Leaders should also consider an individual's ability to participate effectively in the group, which involves a willingness to share with others as well as listen and respond empathetically to others.

With regards to group size, it is recommended that a minimum of five members commit to attending on a weekly basis. A group with fewer than five members is difficult to facilitate because if more than one person is missing, the time spent takes on more of an individual focus than a group experience. Conversely, if a group becomes too large, members who are less assertive or more introverted will be unlikely to share their thoughts and feelings in the group context. A group leader should consider beginning another group if the existing group reaches 9 or 10 regular members.

Group leaders must also attend to the group composition. If there is enough interest and potential members, it is helpful to offer multiple groups with each one focusing on a different developmental stage. For example, leaders could host separate groups for NOPC of preschoolers, elementary age children, preadolescents, and adolescents. Groups often discuss parenting challenges in the aftermath of sexual abuse and share concerns about navigating the particular stage of development.

Although most group members are females (typically mothers), male NOPC can greatly benefit from the group experience. When possible, group leaders can place more than one male in the group so the male feels less alone and can receive support from another male. If there is enough interest, the group leader could also consider offering a group specifically designed for fathers, which may enhance men's willingness to join a group.

In sum, well-equipped leaders, an open group format, and taking care to consider group dynamics set the stage for a powerful and transformative group experience for NOPC. The following section provides an overview of curriculum that is common to groups for NOPC of sexually abused children.

GROUP CURRICULUM

Groups for NOPC provide a blend of psychoeducation about CSA and an opportunity to process their experiences, which includes exploring members' thoughts, feelings, and beliefs. When an open format is used, topics are rotated and tailored to fit the group's needs. Common curriculum components include: (a) exploring initial reactions, (b) learning myths and facts about CSA, (c) sharing thoughts and feelings, (d) improving coping skills, (e) navigating post-abuse life, (f) forgiving, (g) parenting, and (h) supporting the child victim. Handouts, games, experiential activities, and discussion questions can be utilized to explore these topics, which are detailed below.

Exploring Initial Reactions

Group members benefit from sharing with others their initial reactions to their child's disclosure. Members who are new to the group can be encouraged to share their experience of finding out about the abuse. Following the initial shock, parents often recall anger, grief, fear, embarrassment, helplessness, and betrayal. It is powerful for new members to hear others share that they experienced similar feelings.

Psychoeducation

NOPC groups are also a place to provide information. Many NOPC have misconceptions about CSA. Handouts that share the myths and facts of CSA, why children do not typically tell or wait to disclose, and cognitive distortions of sex offenders can help stimulate discussion. It is important for NOPC to learn about the warning signs of abuse, including specific symptoms that are unique to various developmental stages. NOPC can also learn about age appropriate sexual knowledge and normal sexual development. Learning this information helps NOPC understand their children's experiences. Further, it helps them watch for symptoms that may be indictors of further abuse.

Processing Thoughts and Feelings

In addition to information, NOPC need a safe place to explore their thoughts and feelings about their child, the offender, themselves, and the justice system. As discussed previously, NOPC reactions often include shock/denial, anger, sadness, blame, guilt, and embarrassment. They are also likely to hold some faulty thoughts or beliefs about the abuse, their child, or themselves. Some examples include: I should have known he was an offender. No one can be trusted alone with my child. This has ruined our lives. I am a bad parent for letting this happen. A handout listing these and other faulty beliefs can help NOPC process these thoughts and feelings with their fellow group members. Strategies to combat dysfunctional thoughts can be taught to group members (e.g., countering, thought stopping).

Gaining Coping Skills

Besides addressing thoughts and feelings, group leaders can utilize group time to help NOPC learn coping skills. Leaders can demonstrate and provide opportunities to practice deep breathing, guided imagery, and progressive muscle relaxation during group sessions. Leaders can also help members develop a wellness plan that addresses the five areas of wellness: emotional, relational, spiritual, cognitive, and physical. Members can brainstorm daily self-care ideas or choose from a list of ideas. Handouts of self-affirmations can be provided to NOPC so they can practice using them and post in a place where they will see it often.

Navigating Post-Abuse Life

Coping skills are necessary for NOPC as they navigate post-abuse life. Groups can provide a place for members to talk about the changes that they are experiencing personally, relationally, financially, and in terms of stability. Members often struggle with cut off relationships, financial concerns, moving, and involvement in the legal system if the offender is charged or the family decides to press charges in a civil lawsuit. These rapid and extreme life changes can be overwhelming. The group is a place where parents can express their distress without their child having to see or hear them. Although there are no easy solutions, group members can help each other come up with ideas and plans for moving forward.

Forgiveness

Forgiveness is a topic that comes up in many NOPC groups. Although there is a wealth of literature dedicated to the topic of victim's forgiveness of offenders, there is a dearth of studies related to NOPC forgiveness of their child's offender. NOPC should not be pressured to forgive. Instead, it is helpful to explore what forgiveness means, reasons that some forgive, and potential benefits. Forgiveness is very personal and often a deeply spiritual experience. Some NOPC may choose to forgive, while others will not. Leaders can demonstrate support for members regardless of their decision.

Parenting

Along with forgiveness, the topic of parenting frequently arises in NOPC groups. When groups are composed of NOPC with children of similar ages, there is the added benefit of talking about concerns related to a specific stage (e.g., adolescent development and parent-adolescent relationships). Communication is a topic that is applicable to parents with children of any age. Group leaders can provide parents with opportunities to discuss how they communicate with their children. Role plays can be used to practice new communication skills.

When exploring parenting issues in group, discipline is a topic that NOPC have questions about, especially following sexual abuse. They may be tempted to practice permissive parenting or not follow through on consequences out of fear of hurting their child more. NOPC need to be encouraged to maintain clear rules, expectations, and consequences. Although physical discipline is usually not recommended for the sexually abused child, there are other consequences that can be effective.

NOPC can be encouraged to engage in proactive parenting behaviors as well. Examples include: holding family meetings, planning special family time together, and creating regular routines and rituals that enhance predictability and demonstrate love and affection. Parents can be encouraged to try some of the ideas presented in group as homework assignments and report back the following week, which adds accountability.

Supporting the Sexually Abused Child

In addition to learning positive parenting practices, NOPC benefit from learning specific strategies to support their child who has been sexually abused. NOPC help facilitate the healing process when they are able to talk about the abuse openly with their child and communicate that the abuse was not their fault. Many children also need to hear from NOPC that they are not angry at the child. Talking about the sexual abuse is very difficult for many NOPC, and they fear it will make things worse for the child, so they avoid the topic altogether (Ogawa, 2004). Exploring why it is important to talk and specific things that they can say equips NOPC with tools for these conversations.

An acronym that parents can be taught is BRAVE. This teaches parents five specific ways NOPC can communicate support. They are: believe your child, reach out and comfort your child, assure your child that they are not to blame, validate your child's feelings, and encourage your child to talk about what happened (Jinich & Litrownik, 1999). Counselors can role play these supportive actions with group members to help them learn these skills.

Another aspect to supporting their child is learning about common symptoms of sexual abuse which tend to negatively impact one or more domains of wellbeing (e.g., emotional, behavioral, physiological, relational, spiritual, and cognitive/academic) (Goldfinch, 2009; Tomlinson, 2008). Along with knowing how child victims are impacted, NOPC can learn specific strategies to help their children cope. For example, children's narratives revealed that following sexual abuse many children continue to feel afraid (Foster & Hagedorn, 2014b). Parents can ask their children about their fears and employ strategies to help them cope such as making a comfort kit and engaging in guided imagery together (Foster, 2015). Parents can also reinforce strategies that children are learning in counseling (e.g., thought stopping). Additionally, NOPC can be taught how to demonstrate acceptance of their children's feelings by actively listening and avoiding feeling stoppers which shut down open communication (e.g., "There's nothing to be afraid of").

If the NOPC children are receiving therapy utilizing Trauma Focused Cognitive Behavioral Therapy, which is an evidence-based treatment for CSA

(TF-CBT) (Cohen, Mannarino, Berliner, & Deblinger, 2000), group leaders can help prepare members for hearing their children's trauma narratives in family sessions. When NOPC are properly prepared, these family sessions are very powerful and help foster further healing for the NOPC and their children. For further discussion on the trauma narrative family session please see Foster (2014).

Finally, supporting child victims also includes discussing with NOPC ways to keep their children safe in the future. NOPC must learn how to identify warning signs of potential offenders. NOPC must also put safeguards in place to protect their children while utilizing technology since perpetrators frequently use the Internet and phones as a tool to access victims.

In sum, NOPC often enter a group feeling isolated and overwhelmed in the aftermath of their child's sexual abuse disclosure or discovery. NOPC need a place where they can emote and discuss their concerns without their children overhearing them. Group leaders create a group atmosphere that is safe and provides clients with an opportunity to process their experiences and gain new skills for coping and parenting. Group members provide each other with emotional support and understanding. Through exploring the above components with NOPC, group leaders help clients transition from secondary victims to survivors.

SPECIAL CONSIDERATIONS FOR NOPC GROUPS

There are some important topics that may be discussed in group that leaders need to be prepared for as they are complicated and sometimes controversial among group members. They are: parental incest, sibling sexual abuse, and ongoing contact with the perpetrator. Each of these issues will be explored and suggestions for group leaders will be provided.

The first challenge group leaders must be prepared to navigate is that of parental incest. In the screening process, the group leader must verify that the parent who wishes to enter the group is nonoffending, meaning they had no role in the child's abuse. Further, in order to be included in the group, the parent must have responded in a protective manner to knowledge of the abuse once the child disclosed. This includes ending the relationship with the perpetrator and reporting the abuse. This is complicated in cases of incest because it is difficult to determine to what extent the parent was aware of the abuse and if they responded in a protective manner immediately. In some cases, such as ongoing domestic violence, the nonoffending parent may have feared for his/her life and failed to stop the child's abuse or report it to authorities. A NOPC in this situation would benefit from individual counseling to address the complex trauma that they experienced.

After determining an individual meets the criteria for group, leaders need to be prepared for other group members judging the parent for not recognizing the signs of the abuse or behaviors of the offender. Even if these judgments are not verbalized, a group member whose family has experienced parental incest may feel unsupported by fellow members. Discussing these tensions openly and processing them in the group context is recommended. Unless there is evidence to the contrary, the group leader should demonstrate support and belief in the NOPC in this situation.

Similarly, leaders need to be prepared to assist families who have experienced sibling sexual abuse. NOPC of a victim and a child offender experience a significant amount of distress. NOPC are faced with the challenge of securing help for both the sexually abused child and offender (who could be a biological, step, adoptive, or foster sibling) (Foster & Carson, 2013). NOPC in this situation are also susceptible to the judgment of others and group leaders must monitor this. Additionally, group members may share their hate for the offender or desire for the offender to die or be locked up forever. NOPC of a child who has offended may be hurt hearing these things said about perpetrators. They may wonder if group members would want that for their child as well. It is important for group leaders to create a safe environment that allows all voices to be heard. The group leader has an important role in helping members consider other's feelings or perspectives.

Another important consideration that impacts NOPC is the possibility of the child victim resuming contact with the perpetrator. In cases of sibling sexual abuse, family reunification is often a goal following successful treatment. Also, if a case is closed due to insufficient evidence or if a perpetrator receives a not guilty verdict, the child victim may continue to see the perpetrator at school or church. Further, a child may be required to resume visitation if the offender was a parent and has custody rights. NOPC may be completely opposed to resuming contact, especially if they believe the individual was guilty and their child is at risk. This can cause extreme distress for the NOPC. Others may attempt to protect their child from further contact through cutting off family relations, changing schools, or places of worship. NOPC in cases of sibling sexual abuse may be hopeful that treatment was effective but fearful at the same time. Group leaders can help NOPC process these complicated situations.

ALTERNATIVE AND PARALLEL INTERVENTIONS

Although groups are highly effective, some NOPC benefit from alternative and parallel interventions. As discussed in the group components section of the chapter, some NOPC are more appropriate for individual therapy if they have an unprocessed history of sexual abuse, are experiencing clinically significant distress, or if they lack the necessary skills to interact appropriately with group members. Some of these clients are able to move into a group after receiving individual therapy.

An alternative option is for clients to receive a combination of individual counseling (such as a NOPC with a sexual abuse history) and group counseling simultaneously. Group counseling can also be combined with family sessions, which focus on improving family communication, talking openly about the abuse, improving parent-child relationships, and providing the child with an opportunity to share their abuse experience (Foster, 2014). It is important to tailor the treatment to meet the needs of the NOPC and family.

CONCLUSION

To date very few interventions have been developed or evaluated for NOPC, and the specific needs of NOPC are still largely unknown (Jinich & Litrownik, 1999; Tavkar & Hansen, 2011; van Toledo & Seymour, 2013). Empirical literature investigating group interventions for NOPC is in its infancy. Yet, the few existing studies on counseling for NOPC are promising. For example, counseling effectively reduces adults' trauma-related symptoms (Grosz et al., 1999) and positively impacts their children's treatment outcomes (Cohen & Mannarino, 2000; Corcoran, 2004; Deblinger et al., 2001; Feather & Ronan, 2009; Heflin et al., 2000; Silverman et al., 2008). NOPC report that the therapeutic interventions they experienced (e.g., individual counseling, group experience) were valuable for both themselves and their children (van Toledo & Seymour, 2013).

Future research could focus on the impact of the group format and explore what group members experience as helpful to their healing. Group counselors could also be interviewed to identify themes that arise in groups of NOPC. Counselors could provide insight into challenges they experience and how they navigate the complex treatment needs of NOPC.

Counseling CSA victims and their families is both challenging and rewarding (Foster, 2014). Successful treatment is influenced by a number of client factors, including: the gender of the child victim, gender of the offender, level of family functioning, and family's culture (Hunter, 2006). CSA does not always occur in isolation, and some families also experience domestic violence, physical abuse, emotional abuse, and/or neglect (Coid et al., 2001). Dropout is a common problem (Chasson, Vincent, & Harris, 2008) that is influenced by the child's symptom severity, family dynamics (e.g., low SES, single parent, minority status), parental stress and depression, doubt regarding relevance of counseling, and poor therapeutic relationships (Nock, Phil, & Kazdin, 2001). Moreover, NOPC terminate treatment early when they observe increased symptoms in their children (Chasson et al.). Counselors can take a proactive approach by building a strong therapeutic relationship and communicating openly with NOPC about their children's progress. It is important for group leaders to understand the factors that influence the efficacy of counseling interventions and advocate for their clients.

In conclusion, the involvement of supportive NOPC in counseling is recommended for children who have experienced sexual abuse (Lanktree & Briere, 2008). NOPC participation in counseling facilitates positive family relationships in the wake of a devastating experience (McPherson, Scribano, & Stevens, 2012; Sheinberg & True, 2008). Group counseling is a cost-effective, therapeutic form of treatment that leads to positive outcomes for many NOPC.

REFERENCES

Centers for Disease Control and Prevention. (2005). *Adverse childhood experiences study: Data and statistics.* Atlanta, GA: Centers for Disease Control and Prevention, National Center for Injury Prevention and Control. Retrieved from http://www.cdc.gov/nccdphp/ace/prevalence. htm#table.

Chasson, G. S., Vincent, J. P., & Harris, G. E. (2008). The use of symptom severity measured just before termination to predict child treatment dropout. *Journal of Clinical Psychology, 64*(7), 891-904. doi:10.1002/jclp.20494.

Cohen, J. A., & Mannarino, A. P. (2000). Predictors of treatment outcome in sexually abused children. *Child Abuse and Neglect, 24,* 983-994. doi:10.1016/S0145-2134(00)00153-8.

Cohen, J. A., Mannarino, A. P., Berliner, L., & Deblinger, E. (2000). Trauma-focused cognitive-behavioral therapy: An empirical update. *Journal of Interpersonal Violence, 15,* 1203-1223. doi:10.1177/0886260000150 11007.

Coid, J., Petruckevitch, A., Feder, G., Chung, W. S., Richardson, J., & Moorey, S. (2001). Relation between childhood sexual and physical abuse and risk of revictimisation in women: A cross-sectional survey. *The Lancet, 358*(9280), 450-454.

Corcoran, J. (2004). Treatment outcome research with the non-offending parents of sexually abused children: A critical review. *Journal of Child Sexual Abuse, 13*(2), 59-84. doi: 10.1300/J070v13n02_04.

Corey, M. S., & Corey, G. (2006). *Groups: Process and practice* (7th ed.). Belmont, CA: Thomson Brooks/Cole.

Deblinger, E., Stauffer, L. B., Steer, R. A. (2001). Comparative efficacies of supportive and cognitive behavioral group therapies for young children who have been sexually abused and their nonoffending mothers. *Child Maltreatment, 6,* 332-343.

Easton, S. D. (2012). Disclosure of child sexual abuse among adult male survivors. *Clinical Social Work Journal, 12,* 1-12.

Elliott, A. N., & Carnes, C. N. (2001). Reactions of nonoffending parents to the sexual abuse of their child: A review of the literature. *Child Maltreatment, 6,* 314–331.

Feather, J. S., & Ronan, K. R. (2009). Trauma-focused CBT with maltreated children: A clinic-based evaluation of a new treatment manual. *Australian Psychologist, 44*(3), 174-194. doi:10.1080/00050060903147083.

Finkelhor, D. (2012). *Characteristics of crimes against juveniles.* Durham, NH: Crimes against Children Research Center.

Finkelhor, D., Hammer, H., & Sedlak, A. J. (2008, August). *Sexually assaulted children: National estimates and characteristics.* Bureau of Justice Statistics, US Department of Justice. Retrieved from http://www.ncjrs.gov/pdffiles1/ojjdp/214383.pdf.

Foster, J. M. (2015, February). Addressing fear in child victims of sexual abuse. *Counseling Today, 57*(8), 47-51.

Foster, J. M. (2014). Supporting child victims of sexual abuse: Implementation of a trauma narrative family intervention. *The Family Journal, 22*(3) 332-338.

Foster, J. M., & Carson, D. K. (2013). Child sexual abuse in the United States: Perspectives on assessment and intervention. *American Journal of Humanities and Social Sciences, 1*(3), 97-108.

Foster, J. M., & Hagedorn, W. B. (2014a). Through the eyes of the wounded: A narrative analysis of children's sexual abuse experiences and recovery process. *Journal of Child Sexual Abuse, 23*, 538-577.

Foster, J. M., & Hagedorn, W. B. (2014b). A Qualitative Exploration of Fear and Safety with Child Victims of Sexual Abuse. *Journal of Mental Health Counseling, 36*(3), 243-262.

Goldfinch, M. (2009). 'Putting humpty together again': Working with parents to help children who have experienced early trauma. *Australian & New Zealand Journal of Family Therapy, 30*(4), 284-299.

Green, E. J. (2008). Reenvisioning Jungian analytical play therapy with child sexual assault survivors. *International Journal of Play Therapy, 17*(2), 102-121. doi:10.1037/a0012770.

Grosz, C. A., Kempe, R. S., & Kelly, M. (1999). Extrafamilial sexual abuse treatment for child victims and their families. *Child Abuse & Neglect, 24*, 9–23.

Heflin, A. H., Deblinger, E., & Fisher, C. D. (2000). Child sexual abuse. In F. M. Dattilio & A. Freeman (Eds.), *Cognitive-behavioral strategies in crisis intervention* (pp. 166–195). NY: Guilford Press.

Hiebert-Murphy, D. (1998). Emotional distress among mothers whose children have been sexually abused: The role of a history of child sexual abuse, social support, and coping. *Child Abuse & Neglect, 22*(5), 423-35.

Hunter, S. V. (2006). Understanding the complexity of child sexual abuse: A review of the literature with implications for family counseling. *The Family Journal, 14*(4), 349-358. doi: 10.1177/1066480706291092.

Jinich, S., & Litrownik, A. J. (1999). Coping with sexual abuse: Development and evaluation of a videotape intervention for nonoffending parents. *Child Abuse & Neglect, 23*(2), 175-190.

Jones, F., & Morris, M. (2007). Working with child sexual abuse: A systemic perspective on whether children need to tell their therapist details of the abuse for healing to take place. *Journal of Family Therapy, 29*, 222-237.

Lanktree, C., & Briere, J. (2008). *Integrative treatment of complex trauma for children (ITCT-C): A guide for the treatment of multiply-traumatized children aged eight to twelve years.* Retrieved from http://johnbriere.com/articles.htm.

Leckman, J. F., & Mayes, L. C. (2007). Nurturing resilient children. *Journal of Child Psychology and Psychiatry, 48*, 221 – 223.

McCourt, J., Peel, J. C. F., & O'Carroll, P. (1998). The effects of child sexual abuse on protecting parent(s): Identifying a counseling response for secondary victims. *Counselling Psychology Quarterly, 11*(3), 283-299. doi: 10.1080/09515079808254061.

McPherson, P., Scribano, P., & Stevens, J. (2012). Barriers to successful treatment completion in child sexual abuse survivors. *Journal of Interpersonal Violence 27*(1) 23–39.

Nock, M. K., Phil, M., & Kazdin, A. E. (2001). Parent expectancies of child therapy: Assessment and relation to participation in treatment. *Journal of Child and Family Studies, 10*(2), 155–180.

Ogawa, Y. (2004). Childhood trauma and play therapy intervention for traumatized children. *Journal of Professional Counseling: Practice, Theory, & Research, 32*(1), 19-29.

Oz, S. (2005). The "wall of fear": The bridge between the traumatic event and trauma resolution therapy for childhood sexual abuse survivors. *Journal of Child Sexual Abuse, 14*(3), 23-47. doi:10.1300/J070v14n03_02.

Patterson, D., & Campbell, R. (2010). Why rape survivors participate in the criminal justice system. *Journal of Community Psychology, 38*(2), 191-205.

Sheinberg, M., & True, F. (2008). Treating family relational trauma: A recursive process using a decision dialogue. *Family Process, 47*(2), 173-195. doi:10.1111/j.1545-5300.2008.00247.x.

Stauffer, L., & Deblinger, E. (1996). Cognitive behavioral groups for nonoffending mothers and their young sexually abused children: A preliminary treatment outcome study. *Child Maltreatment, 1*(1), 65-76.

Silverman, W. K., Ortiz, C. D., Viswesvaran, C., Burns, B. J., Kolko, D. J., Putnam, F. W., & Amaya-Jackson, L. (2008). Evidence-based psychosocial treatments for children and adolescents exposed to traumatic events. *Journal of Clinical Child and Adolescent Psychology, 37*(1), 156-183. doi:10.1080/15374410701818293.

Tavkar, P., & Hansen, D. J. (2011). Interventions for families victimized by child sexual abuse: Clinical issues and approaches for child advocacy center-based services. *Aggression and Violent Behavior, 16*(3), 188-199. doi: 10.1016/j.avb.2011.02.005.

Tjaden, P., & Thoennes, N. (2006). *Extent, nature and consequences of rape victimization: Findings from the National Violence Against Women Survey*. Washington, DC: U.S. Department of Justice.

Tomlinson, P. (2008). Assessing the needs of traumatized children to improve outcomes. *Journal of Social Work Practice, 22*(3), 359-374.

Tremblay, C., Hebert, M., & Piche, C. (1999). Coping strategies and social support as mediators of consequences in child sexual abuse victims, *Child Abuse and Neglect, 23*(9), 929-945. doi:10.1016/S0145-2134(99)00056-3.

van Dam, C. (2006). *The socially skilled child molester: Differentiating the guilty from the falsely accused.* Binghampton, NY: The Hawthrone Press.

van Toledo, A., & Seymour, F. (2013). Interventions for caregivers of children who disclose sexual abuse: A review. *Clinical Psychology Review, 33*(6), 772-781. doi: 10.1016/j.cpr.2013.05.006.

Welfare, A. (2008). How qualitative research can inform clinical interventions in families recovering from sibling sexual abuse. *Australian and New Zealand Journal of Family Therapy, 29*(3), 139-147. doi:10.1375/anft.29.3.139.

Yalom, I. D., & Leszcz, M. (2005). *The theory and practice of group psychotherapy* (5th ed.). NY: Basic Books.

In: Sexual Abuse
Editor: Olivia Parsons

ISBN: 978-1-63484-509-0
© 2016 Nova Science Publishers, Inc.

Chapter 2

CHILD SEXUAL ABUSE: AWARENESS, SENSITIZATION AND THERAPEUTIC INTERVENTION FOR SCHOOL CHILDREN: INDIAN SCENARIO

P. B. Behere[1,], A. N. Mulmule[2,†], A. P. Behere[3,‡], R. Yadav[4,§] and A. A. Sinha[5,‖]*

[1]Director Research and Development (R & D)
Professor and Head, Department of Psychiatry,
Visiting Professor University of Chester, UK
Adjunct Faculty Georgia Southern University, US
Chairman: Publication Division Indian Psychiatric Society
Jawaharlal Nehru Medical College (JNMC)
Datta Meghe Institute of Medical Sciences (DU)
Sawangi (Meghe), Wardha (Maharashtra), India
[2]MD (Psychiatry), Assistant Professor; Department of Psychiatry,
Government Medical College, Akola, Maharashtra, India
[3]Consultant Child and Adolescent Psychiatrist,
Maine Behavioral Healthcare, Rockland Maine, Clinical Instructor
Tufts School of Medicine, Boston, Massachusetts, US

---

[*] Mobile: +91 9422840552, +91 976540405, email: pbbehere@gmail.com.
[†] M obile: +91 9423657125 email: drakshatamulmule@gmail.com.
[‡] Mobile: 1 -217 622 3429 email: aniruddhbehere@gmail.com.
[§] Mobile: 1-603 443 2134; email: drrichayadav@gmail.com.
[‖] Mobile: +91 9665042070, email: anaghasinha19@gmail.com.

[4]Elmhurst Hospital Center,
Icahn School of Medicine at Mount Sinai, NY, US
[5]Senior Resident, Department of Psychiatry
Jawaharlal Nehru Medical College (JNMC)
Datta Meghe Institute of Medical Sciences (DU)
Sawangi (Meghe), Wardha (Maharashtra), India

ABSTRACT

Nearly 19% of the world's child population, lives in India and children form 42% of the total Indian population. Child Sexual abuse (CSA) in India is an under reported offence but has acquired the nature of an epidemic. Studies across the country have reported a staggering statistic, of every second child being the victim of some or the other form of sexual abuse. Moreover, every fifth child has been reported to have experienced severe forms of sexual abuse. Results of the famous study, the 'Study on Child Abuse India 2007', acted as an eye opener. This suggests the need to increase the awareness regarding CSA and sensitize the prime persons in a child's life viz. parents, teachers and peers, who can bring a definite change in the intervention by reporting it early. Girls are more prone than boys and school going children (7 -13 years) form the most vulnerable age group. There are many unreported and un-noticed cases. On the notion *"axe soon forgets but the tree remembers,"* CSA is considered to be a universal problem with lifelong significant impact nearly in all aspects of life. All CSA victims need therapy and early intervention to prevent later symptomatology. Children tend to face psychological, behavioral and social difficulties. Thus, early intervention is encouraged and is based on notion of *protect, suspect, inspect, collect* and *respect*. The type of therapy to be provided is divided into psychotherapy, creative therapies (including Dynamic play therapy, art therapy or drama therapy), Eye Movement Desensitization & Reprocessing (EMDR). In India, self-help groups of victims & families are another good approach. Several preventive measures established are help lines, awareness programs and community support systems. India has brought several reforms in the existing Indian laws to safe- guard the interest of victims. The most recent of the amendments is the "Criminal Law Act 2013." Finally, the reality lies in the fact that 'everyone can and should report' suspected sexual abuse. Thus considering the magnitude of the problem, this is an effort to provide an overview of Child Sexual Abuse and intervention in the Indian scenario.

Keywords: child sexual abuse, school children, Indian scenario and interventions

INTRODUCTION

India has the largest population of children in the world. It is estimated that one third of India's population is younger than 18 years of age. Several issues that have the potential of deeply affecting a child's wellbeing are rising to the fore. Most recent and predominant of these is child sexual abuse. There is increasing attention and concern towards child sexual abuse in Indian society today as it is known to pose serious and pervasive mental health risks to the child victims as well as their non-offending family members. It is considered not only a violation of a child's body but of the trust implicit in the caregiving relationship. This violation can have a significant impact on how a child initially as a victim and later on as an adult survivor, sees and experiences the world. India is home to nearly 19% of the world's children. The results of a prominent recent study ('Study on Child Abuse India 2007') acted as an eye opener. It was one of the largest surveys conducted in India by the Ministry of Women and Child Development. The study revealed that 53.22% of surveyed children reported having faced sexual abuse, of which 21.90% faced severe forms of abuse. The most vulnerable age group was found to be between 7 and 13 years, i.e., the school going period [1].

DEFINITION

The World Health Organization (2014) defines child sexual abuse as: "The involvement of a child in sexual activity that he or she does not fully comprehend, is unable to give informed consent to, or for which the child is not developmentally prepared, or else that violates the laws or social taboos of society. Children can be sexually abused by adults or other children who are – by virtue of their age or stage of development – in a position of responsibility, trust, or power over the victim" [2].

To simplify, it is the perpetration of sexual acts between an adult and a child or two or more children, forcefully without the consent of the child. The individuals involved can be of the same or the opposite sex [3]. In addition to this, there are sexual acts also referred to as non-contact acts which include sexual remarks directed towards the child by the offender, introduction of objects in the intimate body parts or orifices of the child, exposing the child to pornographic materials, masturbating or deriving other sexual pleasure such as voyeurism. Situations where abuse is caused by a caregiver are all the more traumatic for the child, as he or she is rendered hesitant to seek help since the individual is a man or woman of trust. On the notion "the axe soon forgets but the tree remembers," CSA is considered to be a problem with lifelong consequences impacting almost all aspects of life. Though child abuse is a global issue, in India it is further aggravated by poorly trained police officers who refuse or hesitate to register complaints or encourage the victims to seek a settlement outside the legal system. Low conviction rates and slow criminal and judicial processes, at times lasting for decades add to the problem. The other side of the coin is graver still- victims' families often avoid disclosure due to several factors such as social status, stigma and acquainted offenders. In 94.2% of cases, the offenders were either close friends or relatives [4]. It has gradually become clear that cases are underreported. However, with time both awareness and reporting rates have increased which has led to an increase in the overall prevalence rate in India [5].

DISEASE BURDEN

Sexual abuse in children is considered to be a global problem with a grave burden to society especially on the economic front. It also adds to the burden in various other sectors such as child welfare, the health sector, educational services and the criminal justice system.

Worldwide scenario: The estimate of sexual abuse as reported worldwide is high. Approximately 20% of women and 5 to 10% of men reported experiencing sexual abuse during childhood [6].

Indian scenario: India is reported to be among the top five countries with highest number of sexually abused children in world, along with South Africa, Zimbabwe, U.K and U.S.

The World Health Organization (WHO) survey estimated the overall rate of sexual abuse at any point in life time was one for every ten children [6]. In India, every second child faces sexual abuse in one form or another and every fifth child faces severe forms of abuse. 52.94% of victims were reported to be boys and 47.06% girls [7]. A survey by UNICEF conducted in India from 2005 to 2013 estimated that 10% of Indian girls have experienced sexual violence between 10 and 14 years of age and 30% between 15 and 19 years.

Before Indian girls enter their teenage years, 42% of them will already have faced the trauma of sexual violence [8].

BIOLOGICAL IMPACT IN CASE OF CHILD SEXUAL ABUSE

Psychobiological research has helped us better understand the toxic effects of stress faced by victims of sexual abuse. The trauma of sexual abuse can have an impact not only on brain development but also on physical health, mental health and behavior. It is predicted to reduce brain volume in parts of the hippocampus and the subiculum. This link could help us find better ways to treat survivors of childhood abuse. On persistent exposure to prolonged, severe and unpredictable stress, there is sensitization of neural pathways which leads to activation of fear and anxiety responses [9]. There are also specific signs of dysregulation in the hypothalamic-pituitary-adrenal axis. On prolonged activation of this axis secondary to chronic stress and abuse, there is triggering of cascade of steroid hormones, with the predominant stress hormone being cortisol. Thus, in children in whom the baseline cortisol production is in excess, the baseline for arousal also gets altered [10]. Their neurochemical process suffers dysregulation, especially in the early phase of life when there is ongoing neurogenesis [11]. Such adults, with altered cortisol levels, tend to suffer from Post-Traumatic Stress Disorder, conduct disorder, antisocial personality disorder, depression, and substance abuse in their life time. They are also known to have "Sexual Abuse effect Syndrome" which involves blurring of psychological, social and behavioral boundaries but is difficult to identify [12]. This also has an impact on the immune system of body along with alteration in the metabolic regulatory mechanisms leading to hypertension and cardiovascular diseases [13].

There is a higher risk of multiple health issues including sexual problems, gastric disorders, irritable bowel syndrome, musculoskeletal pain symptoms such as headaches, back aches, muscle aches, fibromyalgia or joint pain and general pain symptoms. There seems to be an increased risk for obesity and eating disorders, particularly bulimia. In addition, non-offending caregivers are often traumatized upon discovery of their children's sexual abuse. They may undergo a spectrum of emotions ranging from anger towards the perpetrator to guilt, self-blame, helplessness, denial, shock, embarrassment and feelings of betrayal. They may also develop serious mental illnesses in due course.

AWARENESS AND SENSITIZATION

With time there has been a definite increase in awareness about the issue because of several reasons- increased focus by the Indian media in response to certain cases, upcoming changes in the law which are being regularly discussed in public and day to day incidences of sexual abuse which are being highlighted. This has resulted in increased reporting of incidences, increased medical facilities for those affected and stringent measures by the government from reforms in existing laws to creating child friendly fast track procedures to minimize the ordeal of the child under trial.

CHANGES IN INDIAN LAW OVER A PERIOD

Several reforms in existing Indian laws have been enacted to safe guard the interest of victims. The most recent of these amendments is the "Criminal Law Act 2013".

1. *Indian Penal Code Law (IPC):* In due course, many shortcomings surfaced in IPC 375 (which defines of Rape) such as restrictive interpretation of penetration, non-friendly and mismanaged trial procedures, poorly trained officials. Thus it was subject to change [14].
2. *Protection of Children from Sexual Offences Act 2012 (POSCO):* It came into force in *November 2012* and defines any individual less than 18 years as a child. For the first time in Indian law, protection for offences such as sexual assault, sexual harassment and pornography are clearly discussed. In addition several reforms are discussed under the Act, the most important being that the reporting of sexual offences by teachers and clinicians is made mandatory and they are liable to punishment in case of failure to do so. The Act states that the legal formalities and proceedings can be carried out after the initiation of medical care by the examining clinician. The Act also provides clearly defined measures to be undertaken by the examining doctors [15].

3. *Justice Verma Committee recommendations:* It was a committee established to suggest ways to provide stringent punishment for sexual offences, in *January 2013*. It had several recommendations right from strict reporting of every cases of child sexual abuse to rigorous imprisonment and protocols for examination of victims [16].

4. *Anti-Rape Bill:* The bill was approved by the Union Cabinet on *12th March 2013*. The salient points as suggested by the bill are: Very strict punishment for rapists and repeat offenders; offences like stalking, voyeurism, disrobing and acid attacks are also included under the bill; the age of consent for sex is increased to 18 years. Repeat offenders can also face the death penalty. The bill defines rape as a crime specific to male gender and only male can be punished for committing such an offence. The first offence will be bailable while a second offence will become non-bailable [17].

5. *Criminal Law (Amendment) Act 2013:* The President of India approved it in *April 2013*. It has a clear definition of the terms involved in child sexual abuse, strict punishments for the offender and treatment of victims made mandatory by all medical personnel, the denial of which is punishable. However the act is gender specific and considers only males liable for punishment [18].

HOW TO IDENTIFY VICTIMIZED CHILDREN?

The risk of mental illness in victims is twice that of the non-abused children. A child suffering from sexual abuse can have varied presentations including Attention Deficit Hyperactive Disorder (ADHD), aggression, anxiety, cognitive/intellectual impairments, conduct disorder, depression, negative parent-child interactions, poor interpersonal relationships/social skills, self-injurious behaviour, social/interpersonal difficulties, substance-related disorders, suicidal thoughts/behaviours, trauma-related problems/ PTSD, and violent/criminal behaviour [19].

Several studies have shown that women who faced child sexual abuse in their childhood are likely to suffer from depression or have twice the risk of attempting suicide compared to those not sexually abused.

INDICATORS OF SEXUAL ABUSE IN VICTIMIZED CHILDREN

- Use of sexuality related statements and behavior with peers, younger siblings,
- Making sexually explicit drawings,
- Sexual interaction and invitation to others,
- Excessive masturbation.

Additionally there are unexplained psychological symptoms in the form of eating disturbances, self-destructive behaviour, self-mutilation, criminal activity, social withdrawal, school difficulties and many more.

HOW TO IDENTIFY PERPETRATORS?

- A person showing undue interest in a child all of a sudden or indulging in inappropriate and excessive, apparently non sexual physical contact (such as hugging, kissing, holding or fondling) despite resistance from the child.
- A person insisting on spending time alone with the child and frequently intruding a child's privacy (walks in on the child in the bathroom).
- A person showering a child with expensive gifts or money for no apparent reason or allowing a child to consistently get away with undisciplined behavior.

ROLE OF PARENTS AND TEACHERS

Along with children, parents and teachers are the appropriate persons to be sensitized about this issue, as they are considered key persons in a child's life. School is the best place to bridge the gap for sexual abuse victims. Parents and teachers should take certain measures for their children such as teaching them to report if they sense somebody's behavior to be inappropriate, even if the person is a known. It is essential to trust one's feelings and empower children to say 'no'. Parents should openly discuss sexual abuse with their children to help them differentiate safe and unsafe touch. Teachers should also stress on sex education in schools and information such as where to seek help in case of an incidence of sexual abuse. It is extremely important for parents and teachers to set up safety plans for children and to collaborate for initiation of regular and appropriate defense measures, as in this case, prevention is the cure [7].

CLINICAL PRESENTATION

The evident changes in a child suffering from some form of sexual abuse are: fearfulness, insomnia, amnesia, day dreaming, enuresis, encopresis, change in behavior in the form of increased irritability, frequent anger outbursts especially towards male members of family, at times abusive, withdrawn, low self-esteem, suicidal, self mutilative behaviors, nightmares, deterioration in school performance, decreased interest in pleasurable activities such as interactive play.

Victims can be exposed to several risk factors which increase their vulnerability for mental illness in future such as single parent or broken homes, faulty parenting, concomitant physical injury/violence, known offender, longer duration of abuse, higher frequency, less family and community support, foster care, multiple perpetrators and disturbed family relationships [20].

CONSENT AND CONFIDENTIALITY

Consent must be obtained not only for a physical examination but also for an interview. Generally a victim can consent if older than 18 years or in most cases, the primary care giver of the child has to provide the consent for an intervention. However, gaining consent can be difficult at times, especially when the perpetrator is a family member or the vested interest of some official authority is involved in the case. In such cases, the child protection authorities may be called in to intervene and help safeguard the child's rights, while also facilitating the medical evaluation.

Before proceeding for therapy, a detailed interview of the victim is essential. It is carried out in an extremely sensitive manner in a neutral atmosphere, taking the child's comfort into consideration. A caregiver (usually the mother) accompanies the child). The presence of other members of the treating team such as social workers, psychologists along with a legal advisor or representative of the law, helps decrease the stress of multiple interviews and benefits the holistic assessment of the situation. Anatomically explicit dolls have served as a familiar medium in expression rather than speech, as they act as a demonstration aid and memory stimulus, and hence are routinely used. A structured interview diminishes bias and helps preserve objectivity. Record keeping of the assessment of any information pertaining to social, behavioral or emotional functioning has to be detailed and comprehensive. A single detailed interview is sufficient if conducted properly. Once an interview is conducted, there are certain aspects which should be kept in mind while treating a sexually abused victim. They tend to pass through various emotions such as despair, guilt, self -blame, anger, flashbacks, fear, anxiety and helplessness. It is preferable to assure the child that they are brave and are being believed for the information they disclose. It is very difficult to be open about such matters and they are neither responsible for it nor do they deserve it. It has to be emphasized at each step that they are not responsible for the assault in any way.

Child sexual abuse accommodation syndrome (CSAAS): This term has been recommended for exploring the difficulty in disclosure of child sexual abuse. After a child undergoes sexual abuse the following events occur; the child is warned to keep the sexual abuse a secret. In the initial period the child feels trapped and helpless. The child's feelings of helplessness and fear about the disclosure being received with disbelief lead to accommodative behaviors. Also, if the child does muster the courage to disclose, and the family or professionals fail to protect the child adequately, it leads to augmentation of the distress and may lead to retraction of the disclosure [21].

Some of the Instruments that can be used in child sexual abuse cases:

1. Child Abuse Potential Inventory [22].
2. Child Sexual Behavior Inventory [23].
3. Children's Impact of Traumatic Events Scale [24].
4. Trauma Symptom Checklist for Children [25].
5. Sexual abuse recognition and nondisclosure inventory (SARDANI) [26].

THERAPEUTIC APPROACH FOR SCHOOL CHILDREN

The most commonly faced query by a clinician is whether all the victims of child sexual abuse need therapy. The premise is to provide therapeutic coverage, as an early intervention tends to prevent later symptomatology. Thus it is highly encouraged and is based on the notion of protect (patient and family safety), suspect (whether the clinical symptoms corroborate with the history presented), inspect (in detail for mental and physical findings), collect (evidences) and respect (right to refuse, privacy and diversity). The type of therapy to be provided is divided into psychotherapy, creative therapies including dynamic play therapy, art therapy or drama therapy and others such as Eye Movement Desensitization & Reprocessing (EMDR).

PSYCHOTHERAPY

Psychotherapy can be delivered from a broad range of theoretical perspectives including behavioral or cognitive, existential or humanistic, gestalt, interpersonal, psychoanalytic and psychodynamic. Commonly, a combination of these therapies is preferred which aims to multiply the benefits of different approaches.

Some specialist practices are:

Trauma-focused approach, which aims to eliminate or reduce the symptoms specific to trauma, such as PTSD and anxiety. Common elements of this approach usually include encouraging the child to express abuse-related feelings, clarifying erroneous beliefs about self or others, teaching abuse prevention skills and diminishing the sense of stigma and isolation [27].

Cognitive Behavior Therapy is a short term therapy where the therapist helps the client develop new coping skills, monitoring thought stream and develop realistic reasoning. It is recommended as a first line treatment for symptoms associated with sexual abuse, however, not suitable for use with very young children.

Group therapy is a powerful way of working with sexual abuse victims as they tend to share feelings and experiences with other victims and thus there is a decrease in shame and stigma faced by victims. Similarly *family therapy* can be considered as an equally important approach, especially in India, where family plays a significant role in life and upbringing of a person. It is considered an ecological approach, as there is focus on the context of problems.

Integrative-eclectic therapy works on the notion of developmental psychopathology. The parent-child attachment is an important component of the adaptive functioning and acts as a strength in adverse conditions for a child [28].

CREATIVE THERAPIES

They tend to use movement in addition to speech, recognizing the connection between our bodies and minds.

Play therapy helps the child express his or her experiences safely. It helps the child to connect abstract thought and concrete experience. Threatening thoughts, feelings and desires can be swiftly expressed by a child and can be easily addressed by the examiner [29].

Trauma-focused play therapy focuses on selection of specific toys which act to re-create elements of the trauma experience and acts as a natural way of gradual exposure. It also gives way to affective discharge and cognitive evaluation.

Non-directive play therapy employs Carl Rogers' person-centered approach to therapy. The child is offered a safe and consistent environment together with a safe and consistent relationship with the therapist. This enables the therapist to work with the child towards resolution [30].

CBT-based play therapy (CBPT) involves both child and therapist in selecting play materials, and play is used to teach skills and alternate behaviors. The therapist offers interpretations, in order to bring conflict into verbal expression [30]. Structured group play therapy is designed primarily to improve the child's peer social interactions.

Filial play therapy is a brief intervention combining play therapy and family therapy. In addition art therapy, drama and psychodrama therapy are grouped under creative therapy.

OTHERS

Eye movement desensitization and reprocessing (EMDR) addresses the factors that contribute to a wide range of problems, looking at past experiences that lie at their root, current situations that trigger dysfunctional emotions, beliefs and sensations, and the positive experience needed to enhance future adaptive behaviors and mental health [31]. The insight regarding the trauma emerges with memory and change is experienced by client [32].

PARENTING INTERVENTIONS

The majority of interventions studied have parent-mediated approaches. Research has shown that the role of the non-offending parent or caregiver ('safe carer') in child sexual abuse cases can be important in producing better outcomes. The outcome of child behavior change can be improved by altering parental behavior. However it is highly important to respect the integrity of the family. Parents need to be empowered to provide vital contribution to their children's growth and development.

PRACTITIONER TRAINING AND SUPERVISION

Clinicians should have some understanding and experience of working with sexually abused children, so they can make sound judgments about the needs of each child and how best to respond and seek the support of others in a team. (Social workers, psychologists etc.).

THE MULTI-AGENCY CONTEXT

Many different agencies are involved in the life of a child, in particular across health, day care and education services. The Government of Maharashtra in India has implemented new guidelines on 10th May 2013 for examination of rape victims under the leadership of *Dr. Indrajit Khandekar*. He has framed questions to be considered while writing a forensic report in sexual abuse cases. These will overcome some of the loop holes and will also be valid in case the victim turns hostile [33]. A Mumbai based NGO called 'Arpan' is the largest registered foundation working on the issue of Child Sexual Abuse with a team of dedicated and skilled professionals since 2006. The vision of Arpan is a world free of child sexual abuse and this foundation has reached out to over 100,000 individuals directly or indirectly.

SUMMARY FOR TREATMENT

- Thus, among well-designed studies, active treatments for sexually abused children demonstrate significant improvements in alleviating aspects of distress, compared to children receiving no treatment [34].
- The most commonly evaluated therapy to-date is CBT, but multiple therapies are the considered more useful.
- The most encouraging findings appear where a parent or guardian was involved in the treatment.
- The therapeutic alliance between the client and the therapist is considered an important relational factor in child psychotherapy [35].

PREVENTIVE APPROACHES

A successful preventive approach is based on the presence of strong family and community connections and supports, creating awareness of healthy parenting practices. In India, self-help groups for victims and families are another good approach. Along with this, parents and teachers can be encouraged to enhance their capability to foster the optimal development of their children and themselves in to the matter.

The Government of India has promoted a lot of schemes, like 24 hour help lines for children in distress, integrated child protection scheme, awareness modules called *"Stay Safe Prevention Educating Children"* for different age groups (5-8, 9-12 and 12-18 years) and a one-day conference on *'Strategies to Prevent Child Sexual Abuse'*. Grant-in-aid Schemes are also run by government to support community based programs.

CONCLUSION

The reality lies in the fact that "everyone can and should report" suspected sexual abuse. However it is finally the personal decision of a survivor to report the abuse. Making reforms in Law can never be the entire answer. There should be sufficient political will to implement it justly. This is a multidimensional issue with varied legal, social and psychological implications. An integrative approach is mandatory. Thus interventions should be tailored on an individual basis which includes involving caregivers to improve compliance, therapeutic alliance among medical personals such as physicians, psychiatrists social workers and psychologists to form an effective team, as well as appropriate legal measures.

Even though the above approaches might not be ultimate solutions, they will surely lead us to towards a working solution.

FUTURE SUGGESTIONS

Treatment manuals for handling child sexual abuse cases for clinicians:

Advantages

- Allow practitioners to draw on an array of different approaches, providing a form of standardization of practice.
- Allow clinicians document details of treatments, its effectiveness, which will in turn inform and potentially improve future manuals and practice.
- It will act as a problem-solving tool, containing techniques to use during therapy, and as a way of ensuring treatment integrity, allowing replication studies to be conducted and determining if changes in treatment advocated in the manual are effective.

Drawbacks

- Practitioners might be hesitant to use them because of various concerns and difficulty in application.
- Using manuals might dehumanize the therapeutic process, obstruct the therapeutic alliance or the focus on the client.
- Limit the practitioner's freedom to exercise the skills.
- It is argued that manuals can become outdated after some time as the research base expands.
  - Regular psychoeducation not only to children but also parents and teachers incorporating measures of self-defense.
  - Proper implementation of existing laws.
  - Recruiting and increasing number of trained officials (especially women officials).
  - Investigating the complaint of sexual abuse immediately after being lodged and at a faster pace.

–   Organizations and community should work to create awareness and report the crime. Media can play a pivotal role in it.

REFERENCES

[1]   Study on Child Abuse: India 2007" (PDF). Published by the Government of India, (Ministry of Women and Child Development). (Available at: http://wcd.nic.in/childabuse.pdf) [Last accessed on 2015 Aug 28].

[2]   Geneva: World Health organization; Child maltreatment. Updated 2014. (Available at: http://www.who.int/topics/child_abuse/en/). [Last accessed on 2015 Aug 09].

[3]   Behere P B, Mulmule A N. Sexual abuse in eight year old girl: Where do we stand legally? *Indian Journal of Psychological Medicine* 2013; 35(2): 203–205. (Available at: www.ijpm.info)/.

[4]   Behere PB, Mulmule A N. Sexual abuse in women and anti rape bill: Lesson to learn from success and failure. *The Health Agenda* 2013; 1: 27-30. (Available at: www.healthagenda.net).

[5]   Behere P B, Mulmule A N. Sexual abuse in children: Where are we heading? The Journal of Mahatma Gandhi Institute of Medical Sciences 2013; 18 (1): 6-11. (Available at: www.jmgims.co.in).

[6]   World Health Organization and International Society for Prevention of Child Abuse and Neglect. Geneva, Switzerland: 2006. Preventing maltreatment: a guide to taking action and generating evidence. (Available at: whqlibdoc.who.int/publications/2006/9241594365_eng. pdf) [Last accessed on 2015 Aug 09].

[7]   Behere P B, Rao T.S.S, Mulmule A N. Decriminalization of attempted suicide law: Fifteen decades of journey. Indian Journal of Psychiatry, 2015; 57(2): 1-3 (Available at: www.indianjpsychiatry.org).

[8]   Singh M M, Parsekar S S and Nair S N. An Epidemiological Overview of Child Sexual Abuse. *J Family Med Prim Care.* 2014; 3(4): 430–435.

[9]   Child Welfare Information Gateway. Understanding the effects of maltreatment on early brain development. 2009. (Available at: www.childwelfare.gov/pubs/issue_briefs/brain_development/brain_deve lopment.pdf) [Last accessed on 2015 Jan 09].

[10] Johnson EO, Kamilaris TC, Chrousos GP, et al. Mechanisms of stress: a dynamic overview of hormonal and behavioral homeostasis. *Neurosci. Biobehav. Rev.* 1992; 16(2):115–30.

[11] Gunnar MR, Fisher PA. The Early Experience Stress and Prevention Network. Bringing basic research on early experience and stress neurobiology to bear on preventive interventions for neglected and maltreated children. *Deb Psychopathol.* 2006; 18: 651–77.

[12] Baes CV, Tofoli SMD, Martins CMS, et al. Assessment of the hypothalamic-pituitary-adrenal axis activity: glucocorticoid receptor and mineralcorticoid receptor function in depression with early life stress—a systematic review. *Acta Neuropsychiatrica.* 2012; 24: 4–15.

[13] National Scientific Council on the Developing Child (NSCDC) (2007a). The Timing and Quality of Early Experiences Combine to Shape Brain Architecture: Working Paper 5. (Available at: http://www. developingchild.net/pubs/wp/Timing_Quality_Early_Experiences.pdf)

[14] [Last accessed on 2015 Feb 02].

[15] Law Commission of India. Proposed Section 373-A Indian Penal Code. New Delhi: Government of India; 1993.

[16] Protection of Children from Sexual Offences Act 2012. New Delhi: Ministry of Law and Justice, Government of India; 2012. (Available at: http://wcd. nic.in/childact/childprotection) [Last accessed on 2015 July28].

[17] Verma JS. Committee Report. New Delhi: Ministry of Home Affairs, Government of India; 2013. (Available at: http://www.mha.nic.in/pdfs/) [Last accessed on 2015 Aug 15].

[18] Anti Rape Bill. The Times Of India. (Available at: http://articles.timesofindia.indiatimes.com/) [Last accessed on 2015 Aug 01].

[19] The criminal law (Amendment) Act 2013. New Delhi: Ministry of Law and Justice, Government of India; 2013. (Available at: http://www.ehitavada) [Last accessed on 2015 April 5].

[20] Cicchetti D. How research on child maltreatment has informed the study of child development: perspective from developmental psychopathology. In D Cicchetti & V Carlson, *Child Maltreatment: The Theory and research on the cause and consequences of child abuse and neglect.* New York: Cambridge University press, 1989: 494-528.

[21] Beitchman JH, Zucker KJ, Hood JE. A review of the long-term effects of child sexual abuse. *Child Abuse Neglect.* 1992; 16(1):101-18. (Available at: www.ncbi.nlm.nih.gov).

[22] Roland et al. The child sexual abuse accommodation syndrome. *Child Abuse Neglect*, 1983; 7 (2): 177–93.

[23] Milner J S, Gold R G, Wimberley R C. Prediction and explanation of child abuse: Cross validation of Child Abuse Potential Inventory. *Journal of consulting and clinical psychology*, 1986: 54; 865-866.

[24] Friedrich, W. N. Child Sexual Behavior Inventory: Professional Manual. Odessa, 1997. FL: *Psychological Assessment Resources*, Inc. (Available at: www.nctsnet.org/nctsn) [Last accessed on 2015 August 29].

[25] Wolfe, V. V., Gentile, C., Michienzi, T., Sas, L., & Wolfe, D. (1991). The Children's Impact of Traumatic Events Scale: A measure of post-sexual-abuse PTSD symptoms. *Behavioral Assessment*, 13, 359-383.

[26] Briere, J. *Trauma Symptom Checklist for Children: Professional Manual.* Odessa, 1996. FL: Psychological Assessment Resources, Inc. (Available at: www.johnbriere.com/) [Last accessed on 2015 August 29].

[27] Faulkner N. Sexual abuse bibliography and references. (Available at: http://www.prevent - abuse-now.com/) [Last accessed on 2015 May 20].

[28] Finkelhor, D. and Berliner, L. Research on the treatment of sexually abused-children – a review and recommendations. *Journal of the American Academy of Child and Adolescent Psychiatry*, 1995; 34(11): 1408–1423.

[29] Egeland B, Jacobvitz D, & Sroufe L A. Breaking the cycle of abuse. *Child development*, 1988; 59(4): 1080-88.

[30] Kot, S., Landreth, G. L., Giordano, M. Intensive child-centered play therapy with child witnesses of domestic violence. *International Journal of Play Therapy,* 1998; 7: 17–36.

[31] Cattanach, A. Introduction to play therapy. 2000. London: Routledge.

[32] Shapiro, F. *Eye Movement Desensitization and Reprocessing: Basic Principles, Protocols and Procedures* (2nd edn). 2001. New York: Guilford Press.

[33] EMDR Institute (2010). Homepage: (Available at: http://www.emdr.com/index.htm) [Last accessed on 2015 Aug 15].

[34] Khandekar I. Forensic medical care for forensic medical care for victims of sexual assault DHR Guidelines. Government of India (Department of

Health Research, Ministry of Health and Family Welfare). (Available at: www.icmr.nic.in) [Last accessed on 2015 Aug 25].

[35] Stevenson, J. The treatment of the long-term sequelae of child abuse. *Journal of Child Psychology and Psychiatry*, 1999; 40: 89–111.

[36] Shirk, S. R. and Karver, M. Prediction of treatment outcome from relationship variables in child and adolescent therapy: A meta-analytic review. *Journal of Consulting and Clinical Psychology*, 2003; 71: 452–464.

In: Sexual Abuse
Editor: Olivia Parsons

ISBN: 978-1-63484-509-0
© 2016 Nova Science Publishers, Inc.

Chapter 3

CULTURAL COMPETENCE AND CHILD INTERVIEWING: UNDERSTANDING RELIGIOUS FACTORS IN CHILD SEXUAL ABUSE INTERVIEWING

Karen L. Haboush[1], PsyD, Anne Meltzer[2], PsyD, Rachel Wang[3], BA, and Narmene Hamsho[4], BA

[1]Clinical Associate Professor
and School Psychology Internship Coordinator,
Graduate School of Applied and Professional Psychology,
Rutgers University, Independent Practice, Highland Park, New Jersey, US
[2]Independent Practice, Scarsdale, New York, US
[3]Doctoral Candidate, Graduate School of Applied
and Professional Psychology, Rutgers University, New Brunswick, NJ, US
[4]Doctoral Candidate, Syracuse University, Syracuse, New York, US

ABSTRACT

Increasingly, the literature on child sexual abuse recognizes the importance of considering cultural factors, including ethnicity and religion, when interviewing and intervening with children. While interviewing children about alleged sexual abuse is always challenging, there is growing acknowledgement of the unique challenges associated with interviewing members of orthodox religious communities. Religious values, including views of sexuality, family structure, and collectivist versus individual norms, may all influence children's reporting. In particular, concerns about the potential for alienating oneself or one's family from the larger religious community may hinder reporting of child sexual abuse. Experiences of religious discrimination and persecution may further contribute to the desire to protect one's religious community from added shame. For these reasons, school personnel, who are mandated reporters, may encounter opposition to their decision to report, despite the increasingly diverse population of public school students, as well as the increase in faith-based schools. Although research within religious communities on child sexual abuse is limited, a growing clinical literature is emerging. This chapter will focus on two historically persecuted groups, Orthodox Jews and Muslims, and the religious values that may enhance culturally competent interviewing skills. Cultural sensitivity requires knowledge and skill in aligning child interviewing techniques with religious values and incorporating community resources: components of forensic interviewing and case examples will be discussed to illustrate these concepts.

Keywords: child sexual abuse, Orthodox Judaism, Muslim Americans, cultural competence, forensic interviewing

Increasingly, the literature on child sexual abuse recognizes the importance of considering cultural factors, including ethnicity and religion, when interviewing and intervening with children (Abu-Baker & Dwairy, 2003; Haboush & Alyan, 2013). Although empirical research is limited, a growing body of clinical literature is emerging which acknowledges the unique considerations associated with interviewing members of religious communities (Gilligan, & Akhtar, 2005; Haboush & Alyan, 2013; Neustein, 2009; Romo, 2013). Religious values, including views of sexuality, family structure, and collectivist norms, may all influence children's reporting of sexual abuse. In particular, concerns about the potential for alienating oneself or one's family from the larger religious community may hinder disclosure (Lesher, 2014). These concerns may be heightened if the alleged perpetrator is a relative (Abu Baker, 2013) or member of religious clergy (Lesher, 2014; Neustein, 2009; Romo, 2013; Pashman & McCoppin, 2015). Experiences of religious discrimination and persecution often contribute to the desire to protect one's religious community from added shame (Gilligan & Akhtar, 2005). For these reasons, health service professionals both within and outside of religious communities may encounter conflict in relation to their legal obligation to report suspected child sexual abuse (CSA) and a desire to protect the community from further shame (Lesher, 2014; Neustein, 2009).

Religious diversity within the United States is rapidly increasing (Pew, 2015b,c). This is partially attributed to declining numbers of European immigrants and increasing numbers of immigrants from predominantly Muslim regions of the world, including Southeast Asia, Sub-Saharan Africa, and the Middle East-North African region (Pew, 2015b,c). Precise figures on religious affiliations are lacking, since the US Census does not collect data on religion; however, as a group, children are especially likely to reflect this diversity since birth rates among immigrants are generally higher (Merrell, Ervin, & Peacock, 2012). United States public schools now have a majority of minority youth (Pew, 2015c). Islam is the fastest growing religion worldwide (Pew, 2015c); recent estimates suggest that approximately 1% of all Muslims reside in the US (Pew, 2015c). Because of a higher birth rate among Muslims, it is projected that the US will have the second largest percentage of Muslims worldwide by 2050 (Pew, 2015c). The US Orthodox Jewish population also has high fertility rates. While Jews comprise approximately 2% of the US population (Pew, 2015b), Orthodox Jews are, on average, younger, marry earlier, have larger families, and continue to have a high birth rate (Pew, 2015a). Thus, given their high birth rates, increasing numbers of Muslim Americans and Orthodox Jewish students are attending both public and private/faith based schools.

This chapter will focus on two historically persecuted groups, Orthodox Jews and Muslim-Americans, and the religious values that may enhance culturally competent interviewing. Both groups have birth rates that are higher than the general US rates (Pew, 2011), rendering understanding of children, families, and child interviewing especially relevant. Culturally, both groups share a strong collectivist emphasis whereby maintaining the well-being of the group is of greater importance than individual needs (Abu Baker & Dwairy, 2005; Lesher, 2014). Unlike those cultures with a more individualistic orientation which stress independent achievement, autonomy, and prioritize individual needs, collectivist cultures place value on the well-being and needs of the larger group or community (Abu Baker & Dwairy, 2003; Dhami & Sheikh, 2000). The larger community includes religious congregations as well as extended family. Children are raised to look within the family for solutions to problems, demonstrate respect toward family members, and in a related vein, avoid actions which might bring shame to the family (Abu Baker & Dwairy, 2003; Gilligan & Akhtar, 2005). As a result, sensitive topics such as sexual matters are viewed as matters to be handled within the family and, in keeping with religious values about the importance of modesty, tend not to be openly discussed in either community (Ali, Liu, & Humedian, 2004; Farih, Freeth, Khan, & Meads, 2015; Haboush & Alyan, 2013; Lesher, 2014).

It is important to note that historically, community cohesiveness has had strong survival value in light of religious persecution and discrimination. The influence of surrounding systems on collectivist cultures aligns closely with Bronfennbrenner's ecological model (Merrell et al., 2012) which considers the impact of surrounding systems (i.e., the media, governments) upon smaller systems (i.e., a family). Concerns about increasing shame may be further heightened if a group is already the target of negative attention and bias (Haboush & Alyan, 2013; McAdams-Mahmoud, 2005). For example, following the terrorist attacks of 9/11 and the more recent rise of ISIS, Muslim Americans have increasingly been targets of discrimination and suspicion (Ali et al., 2004; APA, 2015; Haboush & Ansary, nd). This unfortunate outcome is consistent with a systems-view in which the larger sociopolitical context surrounds communities, towns, schools, and home. The intersection of race, ethnicity and religion further contributes to the experience of multiple types of persecution (McAdams-Mahmoud, 2005), such as that experienced by African-American Muslims, who constitute the largest percentage of native-born Muslim Americans, but experience dual forms of oppression in terms of race and faith (Pew, 2012). Here again, the more insular experience of belonging to a collectivist community may be viewed as an adaptive alternative to the dominant culture's racism and discrimination (McAdams-Mahmoud, 2005).

In addition to the collectivist features of religious communities, houses of worship are also private entities, not monitored by outside bodies to prevent abuse, thus further adding to underreporting of CSA (Romo, 2013). Although prevalence estimates of CSA for the general population have been placed at 1 in every 5 girls and 1 in every 20 boys, rates for specific religious groups are even harder to obtain (Romo, 2013). However, within the Orthodox Jewish community, one study (Neustein, 1977) found rates of sexual abuse as reported by Orthodox females (26%) closely resembled rates for the general population (25%). Additionally, school staff (42%) are more likely to learn of CSA cases than police (13%) and medical professionals (2%) (National Center for Victims of Crime, 2015). Thus, prevalence rates and increased reporting to staff are two additional reasons for school personnel in particular to understand more about CSA and religious influences on reporting.

Although research within collectivist communities on CSA is limited, a growing clinical literature is emerging (Alyan, 2014; Gilligan & Akhtar, 2006;

Neustein, 2009; Romo, 2013). Drawing upon this literature, this chapter attempts to illustrate the manner in which cultural sensitivity and ethical practice on the part of psychologists (APA, 2015, 2010) requires knowledge and skill in aligning interviewing techniques with religious values including family structure, child rearing practices, collectivist norms, and views of sexuality (Haboush & Alyan, 2013). In recognition of the increasingly diverse US population of children attending public and private/faith-based schools, this chapter will: 1) provide basic knowledge of Orthodox Judaism and Islam, 2) develop greater awareness of the relevance of religious factors when interviewing children, 3) improve knowledge of community resources to enhance interviewing, and 4) improve culturally competent interviewing and assessment skills, including forensic interviewing. Case examples will be discussed to further illustrate these points. Throughout this chapter, attention is drawn to the manner in which religion is both a matter of faith and a way of life, comprising the cultural milieu of each community.

ORTHODOX JUDAISM: CHILDREN AND FAMILIES

Introduction

Judaism is a religion that promotes numerous positive values surrounding community, family, education, and charity (Paradis, Friedman, Hatch & Ackerman 1996; Schnall, 2006). However, there are several tenets of the Orthodox Jewish Community that pose unique and significant challenges in child sexual abuse cases and which may conflict with efforts to protect children (Neustein, 2009). For child protective and law enforcement agencies to appropriately conduct interviews with Orthodox Jewish families where sexual abuse has been disclosed, professionals must first obtain basic knowledge about the history and values of the community (Featherman, 1995). The challenges that will be discussed here exist in all stages of an alleged case, from the initial disclosure to the interview process to the psychological consequences. This chapter will focus on issues associated with initial disclosure and forensic interviewing; however, the unique psychological consequences that an Orthodox victim of child sexual abuse faces can be inferred from some of the cultural information provided.

Background

Defining Orthodox Judaism

As with most religions, there is a wide range of religiosity within Judaism. The most commonly used denomination structure in the United States is Reform, Conservative, and Orthodox, with Reform being the least religious and Orthodox being the most (Featherman, 1995). This chapter will focus on the Orthodox community, which is sometimes referred to as the Haredi community. This community is defined by those whose strict commitment to Jewish law and tradition have led to a clear separation from secular values (Lightman & Shor 2002, Schnall 2006; Sublette & Trappler 2000). The values that guide the Jewish way of life are rooted in *Torah* as well as *Talmud*, the legal commentary of the Torah that explains how its commandments are to be carried out. As Featherman (1995, p. 129) notes, "daily life is prescribed in great detail by *Halacha* (rules and norms of Jewish law)." Jewish family values such as gender relationships, norms of child rearing, and attitudes towards sexual violence are dictated by the Torah and Talmud (Featherman 1995; Paradis et al., 1996).

Collectivism

Even though there is vast diversity in observance, culture, and values within the Orthodox community, the different sects all share fundamental beliefs such as monotheism (belief in one God) and collectivism, which is a sense of being part of, and responsible for, the universal Jewish community. As opposed to focusing on individuality and autonomy, Orthodox Jews view themselves as members of the community. As a result, the needs of the group often take precedence over the needs or wishes of the individual members (Lightman & Shor, 2002; Shor, 1998). As Paradis, Friedman, Hatch, and Ackerman (1996) write, "They often strive to separate their communities from mainstream society to maintain their traditional way of life and adherence to their religious values, beliefs, and behaviors (p. 273). A large part of the Orthodox population lives in isolated communities that are guided by values distinct from those of secular society. As Band-Winterstein and Freund (2015) cite from Fass and Lazar (2011), "Despite the typical seclusion-oriented ideology, Haredi society is in constant interaction with the secular environment. The need for professionals in general and social workers in particular is on the increase" (p. 972).

Demographics

It is important that practitioners are exposed to the basic tenets of the Orthodox Jewish people since it is a rapidly growing community in the United States. According to a 2013 Pew Research Study, there are 6.5 million people who identify as Jewish in the United States and 10% of those, or 650,000, consider themselves Orthodox. In the New York City area, 60% of the 1.1 million Jews live in Orthodox homes (Pew, 2013).

Rates of Abuse

Although accurate information about sexual abuse rates is difficult to collect, particularly in insular communities such as the Orthodox Jews, several studies have shown that the rates within the community parallel the rates within the larger United States. Yehuda et al. (2007) surveyed married observant Jewish women and found that 26% had been sexually abused, indicating that the prevalence rates within the Orthodox community parallel the rates in society at large (Neustein, 2009).

Community Values on Gender and Sexuality

In order to understand why disclosure of CSA may be particularly difficult for members of the Orthodox community, it is important to know some basic tenets, particularly the values surrounding gender and sexuality.

Family Structure

In the *Torah*, all persons are equally sanctified in a spiritual and moral sense, but differences in daily duties create a hierarchy of power whereby males have authority and decision-making control. Compared to men, women have less economic power, social standing, legal rights, and religious importance (Biale, 1995):

> Women are primarily responsible for running the household, and men are primarily responsible for financial support and many religious obligations (obligation to study Torah). Men are strongly encouraged to continue religious learning and study throughout their life. The value of study may supersede financial responsibilities, and it is not unusual for a married woman to work to support her husband's study of the Torah... Some couples continue this arrangement for many years and are often

financially supported by parents and other relatives (Paradis, Friedman, Hatch, & Ackerman, 1996, p. 276).

The commandment to "be fruitful and multiply," combined with the desire to make up for the 6 million lost in the Holocaust, leads to large Orthodox families (Featherman, 1996, Sublette & Trappler, 2000). It is not unusual for Orthodox families to have upwards of 8 children (Pew, 2013).

Marriage is a sanctified institution (Paradis et al., 1996). "In traditional society it determines not only the nature of family life and personal happiness of the couple, but also cements the social and economic standing of the families" (Biale, 1984, p. 55). Divorce is often discouraged due to the sanctity of marriage in the Orthodox culture (Paradis et al., 1996).

Modesty and Sexuality

Sublette and Trappler (2000) write, "Social contacts between men and women in the Orthodox communities, especially among Hasidim [Ultra-Orthodox sect], are conducted in a highly structured and protected way (p. 124). Men and women are discouraged from having casual communication with one another, especially Orthodox adolescents. Schools are single-sex. Religious and social events tend to have separate seating based on gender (Sublette and Trappler, 2000). The community rules and values work to prevent inappropriate sexual behavior. A man and a woman are prohibited from being alone in a room together, aside from husband and wife. Any casual contact, including hand shaking, is not permitted between two people of the opposite gender (Sublette and Trappler, 2000).

Females in the community are expected to look and act modestly, referred to as *tzeniut*. Orthodox women cover their hair outside their home, usually with a scarf or a wig. They are expected to wear skirts, as opposed to pants, and have their arms and legs covered (Sublette and Trappler, 2000). Female sexuality is hidden and passive (Biale, 1984).

Children are shielded from exposure to sexually provocative images. Children often do not have access to secular technologies, such as television, movies and the internet (Resnicoff, 2012). They receive little to no sex education (Lesher, 2014). When they are taught about sex, it is usually in regards to sexual transgressions. For example, masturbation and homosexuality are both sins based on the Torah (Greenberg, 2004).

Anti-Semitism, Shonda and the Community Legal Process

Anti-Semitism

The Jewish people have faced persecution throughout history. Hitler's Nazi movement in World War II wiped out around 6 million Jewish people. As Stephen Weinrach (2002) writes, "Hitler's attempt to exterminate Europe's Jewry was only one recent chapter in a long history of malice, or worse, towards Jews" (p. 302). There is understandably a post-Holocaust fear of secular, non-Jewish agencies, such as the United States government, which are seen as having stood idly by while Jews were massacred (Neustein, 2009; Schnall 2006). There is a perception that secular professionals do not understand the Orthodox community's values and lack the ability to communicate with them (Lightman & Shor, 2002). Many in the community believe they survived, and can only continue to survive, by "functioning autonomously and dealing internally with sensitive issues. Jewish people worldwide "share in common vulnerability to attitudes and acts of anti-Semitism. Anti-Semitism may be expressed covertly and unconsciously or blatantly and violently, but whatever the gress, it always resounds with the echo of thousands of years of persecution" (Featherman, 1995, p. 129).

Shonda

As Rabbi Jeremy Rosen (2009) writes, "The more a religion sees itself as being under siege, the more controlling it becomes" (Neustein, 2009, p. xviii). *Shonda,* which is Yiddish for shame, is a guiding principle within the community. *Shonda* is something to avoid. Individuals should not bring *shonda* to their families, and families should not bring *shonda* to the community at large (Paradis). In line with the idea of *shonda,* is the concept of *shalom bayit,* which means peace in the home (Featherman, 1995, Paradis et al., 1996). Due to the community's collectivist-orientation, they are encouraged to prevent any familial discourse from being known to out-groups:

> There is a major fear within the ultra-Orthodox families of the consequences within the community that would follow from disclosing any kind of problem. Among the most critical of these is the awareness that matrimonial prospects (the chances for a good *shiduch*) are greatly affected by a family's reputation: In a community where marriages are arranged, the family's background, as well as the medical and psychiatric histories of its members, are all subject to scrutiny, and affect a family members' potential for a good match. (Lightman & Shor, 2002, p. 318).

There are several commandments that work in accordance with the prevention of *shonda*. Of particular relevance are: 1) the commandment to honor one's parents, 2) the prohibition against gossiping or speaking badly of others (*lashon hara*), 3) the fear of bringing evil fortune on oneself by drawing attention to a human weakness (Sublette & Trappler, 2000, Paradis et al., 1996).

Community Legal Process

Another large guiding principle of the community is the idea of *Hillul hashem*, which prohibits the adjucation of Jews in non-Jewish courts (Featherman, 1995). As a result of Anti-Semitism and Shonda, many rabbinic authorities discourage dealing with secular mental health professionals (Schnall, 2006). The community attempts to solve most conflicts within the Ultra-Orthodox framework (Band-Winterstein & Freund, 2013; Fass & Lazar, 2011). Their desired process is for people to consult with rabbinic authorities before reporting to secular authorities (Schnall, 2006). Rabbi Shlomo Gottesman insisted that only Orthodox rabbis can determine what constitutes "reasonable suspicion"; therefore, he declared, no one may report a [digression] to authorities without first receiving rabbinic permission (Lesher, 2014). Reporting illegal activity to secular authorities means the disclosure of private problems, which stands in opposition to the desire to prevent issues from leaving the community (Lightman & Shor, 2002).

Issues with Disclosure

For Child Victims

A delay or lack of disclosure is common among all children who are victims of sexual abuse and Orthodox children are no exception. All of the aforementioned tenets of the community pose potential challenges for initial disclosure. Biale (1984) explains that "In the patriarchical family, women rely on fathers, brothers, and husbands to be their protectors. The family is the structure protecting women from sexual exploitation by outsiders. If an "insider" – father, brother, uncle, or brother-in-law-himself becomes a threat, seducing or even raping a woman within his own family, she has little protection" (p. 180). This concept also applies to situations in which the rabbi is the perpetrator, since the rabbi is considered the leader and protector of the entire community (Featherman, 1995). The same values that promote modesty and hinder open sexuality are the values that often effect disclosure in sex abuse cases. "Often abusers will make a female victim believe that she was responsible for the abuse because she did not dress modestly enough" (Featherman, 1995, p. 136). For boys, the understanding of homosexuality as a sin makes disclosure particularly shameful (Greenberg, 2004). An older child might be concerned that disclosure would disrupt peace in the home (*shalom bayit*) and would bring shame (*shonda*) upon his or her family within the community (Schnall, 2006). The commandment against *lashon hara* (gossip) combined with the value of respecting elders, makes it incredibly difficult for children to speak out against their perpetrators (Featherman, 1995).

For Adults Made Aware of Child Abuse

Several factors also contribute to the delay or lack of reporting to secular authorities by the adults in the community that become aware of alleged sexual abuse. This could include the child's non-offending parent, older siblings, other relatives, school personnel, and religious leaders. Sarah Silverman writes, "Before Orthodox Jewish victims seek help, they must not only make decisions about their own and their children's safety and welfare, they also have to overcome deep personal, cultural, and communal barriers" (2014, p. 5). When the perpetrator is the father, the mother may fear emotional, and possibly physical, repercussions. She will get pressured to stay in the marriage. She fears the husband will not grant them a *get* (divorce) (Silverman, 2014). On the one hand, she wants to protect her children from a sex offender, but on the other hand, she knows that public knowledge of this will bring *shonda* (shame) upon her and her children (Schnall, 2006). For example, the children may not be allowed to continue attending their *yeshiva* (school) and they may run into trouble when their arranging a marriage for their children. As mentioned above, marriage is sanctified and defines one's social status in the community. An adolescent is examined with close scrutiny during the marriage arrangement process. Knowledge that the family failed to keep their familial issues within the home would not fair well for the children's future prospects (Schnall, 2006, Sublette & Trappler, 2002).

Even when an adult in the community discloses to the rabbinic authorities, the disclosure will often times not reach secular authorities. Neustein (2009) writes, "*Shonda,* which has traditionally served as a useful mechanism for social enforcement of community values, norms, ethics, and propriety, has a disadvantage: fear of public shame can loom so large in the eyes of the Jewish community that many of its leader and lay members will deny the existence of a scandalous secret like sexual abuse" (p. 4). In some cases, the rabbis will actually side with the perpetrator and blame the victim for bringing about *shonda* or committing the sin of *lashon hara* (Lesher, 2014). Lesher (2014) provides an example of this from a recent case: "When Rabbi .....was accused and later convicted of repeatedly raping a minor, the rabbis of his Satmar community launched a fundraising campaign to pay his legal bills, simultaneously plastering shopping malls with posters depicting his victim as a missile aimed at the heart of the community" (p. 78). It is important to note that this reactionary stance cannot be applied to the community as a whole. In fact, there have recently been many more agencies, as well as rabbis, within the community who are recognizing child abuse as a serious issue and taking matters into their own hands (Neustein, 2009).

FORENSIC SEXUAL ABUSE INTERVIEWING WITH ORTHODOX JEWISH CHILDREN

Conducting forensic sexual abuse evaluations with Orthodox Jewish children poses unique challenges, which have received little attention in the literature on child sexual abuse. The purpose of these evaluations is to ask questions in an open-ended manner that will help children accurately communicate with detailed descriptions what, if anything, has happened to them (APSAC Practice Guidelines, 2012). It is therefore imperative that forensic interviewers obtain cultural competence with regard to Orthodox Jewry in order to approach the interview process with sensitivity and to maximize the amount of accurate information obtained from the child. The purpose of this section is to raise awareness of potential issues to consider when interviewing Orthodox children; this section is not intended to establish professional standards for forensic interviewing or to constitute legal advice.

The issue of interviewer bias is an important aspect when one is conducting a culturally competent forensic interview (Abney, 2002; Elwyn, Tseng, & Matthews, 2010; Pence, 2012; Poole & Lamb, 1998). It is recommended that an interviewer "engage in an ongoing process of self-reflection regarding personal responses and possible biases in order to cultivate greater cultural awareness and avoid stereotyping" (APSAC Practice Guidelines, 2012). It is also necessary for the interviewer to be aware of possible biases in order to remain neutral and objective throughout the forensic interview process (Abney, 2002; Caudill, 2006; Koocher, 2006). It is not unusual for an interviewer or therapist to feel confusion regarding some of the Orthodox customs (Sublette & Trappler, 2000). As an interviewer, one needs to understand that culture plays a role in perceptions, behaviors, sex roles, interactions, expectations and modes of communication (Abney, 2002).

Efforts have been made in the past few decades to standardize the interview process with the development of protocols (Lamb, Hershlowitz, Orbach & Esplin, 2008; Saywitz, Lyons & Goodman, 2002). Lamb et al. (2008) define a protocol as a "flexibly structured guide incorporating a wide range of strategies believed to enhance the retrieval and accurate reporting of information about experienced events." Although there is no one protocol that every forensic interviewer follows, there is agreement that the forensic interview is an important component of the investigative process and that "forensic interviewers should use open-ended questions to support children's ability and willingness to describe remembered experiences and to elicit details more productively (Hershkowitz et al., 2007; Newlin et al., 2015; Orbach, Shiloach, & Lamb, 2007).

Although some of these protocols stress the importance of cultural competence, most do not offer specific strategies for the interviewer who is faced with interviewing a child from a different culture (Fontes & Faller, 2007). Fontes (2005) emphasizes that "Forensic interviewers and investigators must consider the influence of culture on perception of experiences, memory formation, language, linguistic style, comfort with talking to strangers in a formal setting, and values about family loyalty and privacy when questioning children and evaluating their statements. Interviewers should, therefore, make concerted efforts to educate themselves about the child's culture (Fontes & Faller, 2007) and "learn as much as possible about the child's cultural background, practices and language proficiency prior to the interview, and adapt the interview accordingly" (APSAC Practice Guidelines, 2012). More specifically, the interviewer should become knowledgeable about the family's "child-rearing practices, sex roles, family structure, religious beliefs, worldviews, community characteristics and levels of acculturation or assimilation (Abney, 2002). All of these issues are particularly important when interviewing Orthodox Jewish children who have alleged sexual abuse.

In recent years, more cases of sexual abuse and other familial issues within the Orthodox community are being brought to the attention of secular authorities (Schnall, 2006) despite this being in opposition to Jewish Law (Lightman & Shor, 2002). Forensic interviewers are therefore encountering many more children to evaluate from this culture who are alleged to have been sexually abused. Based on the tenets of Orthodox Judaism discussed earlier in this chapter, one can easily understand why familiarity with this culture and its religious customs are necessary to conduct an optimal interview. If an interviewer has no knowledge of the Orthodox culture, it would be important to find out as much as possible about relevant cultural values prior to beginning the forensic interview process (Fontes & Faller, 2007).

Stages of Interviewing: Rapport Building

The forensic interviewer typically proceeds through three stages when conducting a sexual abuse interview(s): the Rapport-Building Phrase, the Substantive Phase, and the Closure Phase (APSAC Practice Guidelines, 2012; Lamb et al., 2008; Newlin et al., 2015). The rapport-building phase consists of introducing oneself to the child, determining if the child knows why they came, inquiring as to whether someone told them what to say to the interviewer, interview instructions, explaining the method of recording the interview, discussing the importance of telling the truth versus telling a lie, general questions about the child's home and school life, eliciting a narrative description of a non-abuse event in their life (i.e., asking them to give detailed information about a topic such as what they did during the summer vacation), and assessing their episodic memory (Newlin et al. 2015). The substantive phase consists of eliciting a narrative description of the sexual abuse in response to open-ended questions (i.e., "Tell me what happened"). If the child is reluctant to speak, focused questions and direct prompts should be used to obtain as much detail about the abuse as possible (i.e., asking "who," "what," and "where" questions). In this phase the interviewer should be attempting to rule out alternative hypotheses such as coaching, fabrication, inappropriate questioning, etc.

The closure phase consists of asking the child if they have any questions, thanking the child for their efforts, explaining what the next step will be in the process, and spending some time talking about a non-threatening neutral topic. (APSAC Practice Guidelines, 2012; Faller, 2007; Lamb et al, 2008; Newlin et al., 2015, Poole, 1998).

Cultural competence has an impact on each of these stages, and particularly for Orthodox Jewish clients. During the rapport-building phase, the interviewer spends time establishing a sense of comfort between the child and the interviewer. This can be accomplished by talking to the child at their developmental level and asking open-ended questions about topics that are neutral and unrelated to the allegations such as school, birthdays, holidays, activities, etc. (APSAC Practice Guidelines, 2012, Lamb et al., 2008). Family routines, customs, and cultural and religious beliefs need to be ascertained by the interviewer and understood within the context of the evaluation (Tishelman, Newton, Newton, Denton, & Vandeven, 2006). For example, one needs to know that Orthodox Jewish children typically do not know their American birth dates, schools are segregated by gender (Silverman, 2014), children attend school Sunday through Thursday, and do not attend school on Friday and Saturday, as those are the days of the Shabbat observance (Sublette & Trappler, 2000). Additionally, they do not play organized sports (Schnall, 2006) and do not celebrate Halloween, Fourth of July, Thanksgiving, and other secular American holidays. Instead, they celebrate or observe many holidays of importance that might be unfamiliar to the interviewer such as Sukkos, Purim, and Shavuos to name a few (Paradis, Friedman & Hatch, 1996). Furthermore, many do not have televisions in their homes (Sublette & Trappler, 2000), have limited or no access to computers, and have little or no exposure to sex education (Lesher, 2014). Without exposure to television, children likely do not have knowledge of current popular characters that most children outside of this community are familiar with such as *Dora the Explorer* or *Thomas the Tank Engine*. One would therefore need to avoid referring to these characters in rapport-establishing questions and discussions.

Another area that interviewers must be knowledgeable about is the child's use and understanding of the English language (Fontes & Faller, 2007). This is often ascertained by asking the child to give a narrative about a non-threatening event in the past or a topic the child has brought up during this rapport-building phase. This allows the child to provide a forensically detailed description of a non-abuse event and enables the interviewer to begin to understand the child's linguistic ability and style (Newlin et al., 2015). However, for many Orthodox Jewish children, Yiddish is their first language, and the child may have difficulty providing narratives in English, which is most often their second language (Schnall, 2006). The interviewer must be aware of this cultural difference and not assume that a child who struggles to provide a narrative is not competent in his or her expressive language skills. For a child with very little or no understanding of the English language, the interviewer should conduct the interview in Yiddish or use a neutral and experienced professional interpreter who is fluent in Yiddish to help interpret interview questions and responses for both the child and interviewer throughout the evaluation (Elwyn et al. 2002;Fontes & Faller, 2007).

There are also common Yiddish words that the interviewer should be familiar with, as they come up often during an interview of an Orthodox Jewish child. Examples of some words would be: *"Yeshiva"* for school, *"tuchas"* or *"tushie"* for buttocks, *"tatty"* for father, *"bubbe"* for grandmother, "*zaide*" for grandfather, "*tante*" for aunt, "*feter*" for uncle, "*shul*" for temple, "*keppe*" for head, "*daven*" for pray, "g*oy*" for a non Jewish person, "*pupik*" for belly button, and "*potch*" for a light hit. Knowing many of these words will help the interviewer obviate the need to ask for translations by the child and thereby avoid the child feeling frustrated. The following case vignette illustrates the importance of being aware of religious observances and common Yiddish words. All case material has been altered to protect confidentiality:

> A six year old boy described being abused by his "Feter Moishe" when he went to his house where his "Tante Rivka" took care of him afterschool. He said the first time was during "*Succos*" and the other time was right after "S*habbos*" ended. He said that his "*Feter*" pulled down his pants and put his thing in my "*tushie*." He said his shirt and *tzistzis* were still on.

One would need to know that "Feter" means uncle and "Tante" means aunt in order to be clear about important details of this child's disclosure. Knowing that "*Succos*" is a holiday that occurs in the fall, that "*tzistzis*" refers to the knotted fringes that Orthodox Jewish males wear under their shirts, and that "*Shabbos*" is the weekly observance from Friday at sundown through Saturday at sundown would help one to understand the timeline and additional details provided by this child.

It is also important for the interviewer to be mindful of the fact that many Orthodox Jewish children and their families have had little or no exposure to secular society and are not used to talking to strange people who are outside of their community (Sublette & Trappler, 2000). This can result in a greater sense of discomfort and mistrust of the interviewer for the children and their families (Lightman & Shor, 2002). The interviewer may need extra sessions to allow the child to develop enough of a sense of trust to open up about sexually abusive experiences.

During the rapport-building phase, it is strongly recommended that the interviewer give interview instructions such as telling the child not to guess or make up an answer (APSAC Practice Guidelines, 2012; Faller, 2007; Lamb et al., 2008; Newlin et al., 2015). They should also be told the importance of telling the truth and that it is okay if they don't know the answer. Additionally, children should be told that they should ask for clarification if they do not understand the question and given permission to correct the interviewer when an erroneous statement is made (APSAC Practice Guidelines, 2012; Lamb et al., 2008; Newlin et al., 2015). It is especially important to incorporate these instructions in the process when interviewing Orthodox Jewish children who may not understand many of the questions and are not used to correcting adults. They are raised to show deference to authority and giving them permission to do this will often help them comply with this directive and not feel they have to be deferential to the interviewer (Sublette & Trappler, 2000). This will also help to lessen the degree of suggestibility during the interview.

Middle Phase: Obtaining a Narrative

The next phase of the forensic interview involves obtaining a narrative description of the alleged events using a free narrative style. This entails asking questions asked in an open-ended manner followed by open-ended prompts (Lamb et al., 2008; Lyon, 2012). However, an Orthodox Jewish child may be particularly anxious or embarrassed due to cultural values such as *tzeniut*, a word which means modesty. The concept of sexuality is generally not talked about at home and this topic is not part of their school's curriculum. Instead, the rule of modesty is emphasized, which likely results in victims of sexual abuse feeling especially shameful about the sexual contact on their bodies and, in some cases, the sexual contact they are forced to have on the offender's body (Featherman, 1995). This can result in greater difficulty and, at times, complete unwillingness to describe acts of sexual abuse with an interviewer who is a stranger.

This reluctant behavior may require the interviewer to use a more focused approach, as well as other options, such as interview aids. These interview aids might include anatomically detailed dolls or focused drawings where the child is asked to draw what happened to them (Kuehnle, 1996; Pipe & Salmon, 2009). The drawings may not only be a more comfortable way for the child to reveal what happened, but it also may provide the child a stimulus to generate details of the sexual abuse without having to answer a lot of questions (Faller, 2007). Although the use of these interview aids can be risky if children are allowed to freely play with them, there are potential advantages of using them in situations where the interviewer needs clarification of the sexually abusive body contact. Dolls are also helpful for children who are having difficulty expressing themselves verbally due to language issues, as well as feelings of fear, embarrassment and shame (Kuehnle & Sparta, 2006; Pipe & Salmon, 2009). The child should, nevertheless, be encouraged to verbalize what happened to whatever extent they can either before or during the use of these interview aids (Kuehnle, 2011). The use of a focused drawing was helpful in the following case:

> During a forensic interview, a seven year old girl Orthodox Jewish girl disclosed that something had happened to her, but did not want to verbalize it because she was too embarrassed and did not want to make her mother feel sad. She further said that she didn't want anything bad to happen to her family. She willing agreed to draw pictures of what happened to her and drew a very clear and compelling picture of her father dressed in Hasidic clothing with his pants partly down and a girl with her dress up and underwear off. The child explained that in the drawing the girl and her father were lying on his bed and the girl was saying, "Please stop. Don't do this anymore."

The following case illustrates how the use of a few interview aids helped a child open up about her abusive experiences:

> A nine-year-old Orthodox Jewish girl was allegedly abused by her father and said she did not want to tell what happened because she was too afraid of what might happen to her. She eventually verbalized what happened while demonstrating with anatomically detailed dolls. One of the things she described was her "*tati shterking*" her, but was unable to translate what that meant in English. Using the dolls and a focused drawing, it became clear that she was referring to being poked in her vaginal area with his finger. She also disclosed that she was told that she would be given candy if she didn't tell.

The interviewer should also establish what names the child uses for their genitalia and other sexual body parts. Many will refer to their buttocks as a "*tuchas*" or "*tushie,*" but they often don't have words for their other private parts. This is another reason why use of the dolls can be helpful; it enables the interviewer to have clarity as to what body part the child is referring to in their description of the abuse. However, the interviewer must be trained in the specific ways the dolls can be used; otherwise they can lead to misinformation (Faller, 2007; Lamb et al.; 2008, Newlin et al., 2015).

Closure Phase

Cultural competence has some impact on the closure phase of the interview because, again, the interviewer needs to come up with an appropriate neutral topic to converse about at the end of the session. One needs to avoid choosing a topic that would be unfamiliar or uncomfortable for the child.

Mothers, Gender Roles and *Shonda*

Another component of the forensic interview involves interviewing the child's caretakers and the person accused of abusing the child. As with the child, family customs, routines and cultural and religious beliefs need to be understood within the context of the adult's interview (Ayoub & Kinscherff, 2006, Tishelman et al., 2006). With Orthodox Jewish families, one may encounter reticence from the mother to answer questions about her knowledge of the sexual abuse because of fear that she is betraying the community. The mothers are often reluctant to discuss their marital relationship and other family problems with the interviewer and one needs to be sensitive to this (Sublette & Trappler, 2000). They often express guilt about not protecting their child and not reporting the abuse as soon as they suspected it. Sometimes this reticence is due to the pressure they receive from rabbis in the community to not participate in the investigation or their general lack of trust toward secular society (Lightman & Shor, 2002). Many wonder whether non-Orthodox professionals are able to understand and be sensitive and respectful to their values and customs (Paradis et al., 1996). Therefore, what may be viewed as neglect on the part of the mother for not bringing her knowledge of the abuse to the authorities, has to be seen in the context of her religious environment. Mothers frequently express realistic fears that if the community becomes aware of the sexual abuse, their child will no longer be allowed to attend the *Yeshiva* and their child's prospects for marriage will be diminished when it comes time to arrange their marriage (Sublette & Trappler, 2000). They may also feel pressured to stay in the marriage as divorce is often discouraged due to the sanctity of marriage in the Orthodox culture (Paradis et al., 1996) and because it brings with it an element of shame and disappointment (Silverman, 2014).

A mother whose young daughter alleged sexual abuse by her father stated:

> "I wanted to do the right thing and stay in the marriage. I did everything I could to please my husband even though he was violent towards me and may have sexually abused my child. I don't want to say more than I have to. I need to protect my children in the community or they will all be thrown out of school and no one will want to talk to us."

Another mother who wanted a divorce and was beholden to her own parents stated: "My parents know my husband is disturbed, but they do not believe in therapy. Their philosophy is, 'God thinks you should be able to handle a dysfunctional husband and you can be helped by spiritual talk and being positive. They told me if I dressed better and cooked better, my husband would not be doing the things he is doing." I know my husband is colluding with his rabbi and they are both trying to control me and make everyone think I am the crazy one and not him."

Males and Gender Roles

When interviewing an Orthodox Jewish man as part of one's forensic evaluation, the interviewer again needs to be mindful of specific customs within the community. For example, an Orthodox Jewish man will avoid eye contact with another woman and is not permitted to touch a woman other than his wife (Band-Winterstein & Freund, 2015). Therefore, a female interviewer should not attempt to shake hands with any Orthodox man involved in the investigation (Paradis & et al., 1996; Sublette & Trappler, 2000). A female interviewer should maintain a reasonable seating distance from the male she is interviewing and dress conservatively out of respect for the rules of modesty (Band-Winterstein & Freund, 2015; Paradis et al., 1996; Sublette and Trappler, 2000). In many cases, the fathers may have very little knowledge about their children's lives, as it is the mother's responsibility to run the household while the father attends his religious learning (Featherman, 1995; Paradis et al., 1996). If the father is the alleged offender and the parents are estranged from each other in a conflict ridden marriage, it is not unusual for each of them to secure the support of opposing rabbis in the community (Lesher, 2014; Lightman & Shor, 2002) much the same way non-orthodox individuals obtain lawyers. A father who was accused of abusing his son and was eventually exonerated stated:

"When my son was young, a rabbi my ex-wife knew in the community got involved. He said I could see my son with the mother present. Eventually, this rabbi said I could see my son for a few hours a week, but it had to take place in his home. Then another rabbi in the community, who believed I was innocent, began helping me. He said he would testify in court against the mother because he felt she was not a good mother."

The above illustrates that conflicts and issues are often solved by rabbis and other community authorities (Greenberg & Wiztum, 1994) and that members will lead their lives adhering to a strong rabbinical authority (Paradis et al., 1996).

Legal and Professional Obstacles

In addition to encountering some resistance from the child's caretakers to be forthcoming, one might also encounter some resistance from school personnel, and therapists within the Orthodox community, as they too fear reprisal from the community and are reluctant to get involved with secular professionals and the court. Rabbis may encourage parents to seek help from an Orthodox Jewish therapist as they want a therapist involved who adheres to the norms of the community (Paradis et al., 1996). When asked for information about a child undergoing a forensic sexual abuse evaluation, an Orthodox therapist not trained in the area of sexual abuse stated:

"I know this could not have happened. The rabbi told me he is a good man and that he is very religious and respected in the community. I know he is a good father and he would never hurt his child... The rabbi said the mother is making this up and I agree that she is... I told the mother that her child was not abused and she must do something to stop the investigation."

Many therapists, rabbis, and school officials, however, are very concerned about the safety of the alleged victims and will want to work with secular professionals and aid the investigation in any way they can (Paradis et al., 1996). There is a growing awareness of sexual abuse in these communities and more religious leaders are becoming activists in the plight to protect child victims and have these cases adjudicated by our justice system (Lightman & Shor, 2002).

Ultimately, an integration of resources within the Orthodox and secular communities is needed to best serve children. Interviewers must utilize both written resources and direct contact with members of this community to gain enough knowledge to sensitively conduct a culturally competent interview. Members of these cultural communities, including religious leaders, need to be educated about the process of the forensic investigation in sexual abuse matters and, in turn, professionals need to be educated about the differing cultures. Cultural competence does not happen automatically or easily Faller (2007).

MUSLIM AMERICANS: CHILDREN AND FAMILIES

Introduction

Islam is a monotheistic religion that originated in the seventh century. Today, Islam is the fastest growing religion in the world and in the United States (Pew, 2015b). Muslim Americans are a racially and ethnically diverse group. Following the 9/11 terrorist attacks, discrimination and bias against Muslim American has increased sharply (Haboush & Alyan, 2013; Pew, 2011). Despite documentation of many Muslim's acculturation to American life, many Muslims also look to their communities in response to discrimination and a desire to preserve Muslim religious practices and way of life. Increasingly, children also attend private Islamic schools designed to both promote religious practices and an Islamic way of life.

Defining Islam

Islam is the Arabic word for "surrender" which refers to surrendering to God's (*Allah's*) will. The five pillars of Islam provide a framework for followers that include the following: belief in only one God (*Allah*); praying five times a day; fasting during the holy month of Ramadan; giving charity to those in need; pilgrimage to the holy place of worship (Kaaba) in Mecca. Followers of this monotheistic religion are known as Muslims and their beliefs, values, and codes of behavior stem from two sacred texts, the *Qur'an* and the *Hadith*. The *Qur'an* is the religious text of Islam, which Muslims believe to be the word of God that was dictated to the prophet Muhammed (*pbuh*)1, and identifies itself as a book of guidance. It is written in Arabic, although Muslims originate from many countries. In addition, the *Hadith* is a collection of quotations from the prophet Muhammed (*pbuh*) that serves as moral guidance for Muslims. Sunnis and Shiites comprise two of the major sects within Islam, and differ from each other in terms of beliefs about the prophet Muhammed's (*pbuh*) successor, and interpretation of certain parts of the *Qur'an*. Although degrees of religiosity may differ among Muslims, surveys indicate that many Muslims endorse a relatively high degree of religious observance (Pew, 2011).

Collectivism

Islam emphasizes the good of the community. While encouraging individuals to meet their needs and interests, this should not occur at the expense of the group or community and actions which may be bring shame to the community are discouraged. The family and religious congregation constitute the most central core of an observant Muslim's community. Family includes extended family and elders are afforded considerable respect. Thus, power is based on age and gender (Gilligan & Akhtar, 2005).

Demographics

Islam is the fastest growing religion in the world and in the United States (Pew, 2015b,c). Muslim Americans comprise approximately 1% of the world's Muslim population (Pew, 2011). Estimates suggest approximately 1 million Muslim American children reside within the US. In terms of projections, it is expected that: 1) the number of Muslims will almost double by 2030 to roughly 1.7% of the total population, and 2) the US will have the second largest population of Muslims worldwide by 2050 (Pew, 2015b,c). The majority have origins in South Asia, Middle East/North Africa, or sub-Saharan Africa. Twenty five percent of adult Muslim Americans arrived in the US since 2000, 63% first generation immigrants, and 15% second generation (one or both parents born outside the US). Islam was originally brought to the US by African slaves; thus, the largest percentage of native-born Muslims are African American (Pew, 2011). Statistics show that while the majority of Muslim Americans identify as practicing Islam (Pew, 2011), they are also characterized by considerable variability in terms of the branch of Islam practiced, country of origin, acculturation, and degree of religiosity to name a few (Haboush & Ansary, nd). Sunnis and Shiites comprise two sects of Islam, though there are others, which differ in terms of views of the prophet Muhammed's (*pbuh*) successor, certain daily practices, and interpretations of the *Qur'an*.

Rates of Abuse

Data on rates of CSA among Muslim Americans are lacking and cases are likely underreported (Gilligan & Akhtar, 2005). Rates in larger society generally reflect that 1 out of 5 girls and 1 out of 20 boys are victims of CSA (National Center for Victims of Crime, 2015) and the majority of perpetrators are known to the child. However, the potential that CSA among Muslim youth is underreported must be considered in light of the cultural propensity to avoid actions which might be viewed as shaming the family (Abu Baker, 2013; Abu

Baker & Dwairy, 2003; Gilligan &Akhtar, 2005). Alyan (2014) reported that in a survey asking adult Arab American women about CSA, all the respondents were Muslim and reported histories of sexual abuse perpetrated by family members. Over half reported the onset of CSA began before age 8 and family members were the majority of perpetrators (Alyan, 2014). Thirty-three percent of the sample reported they were told to keep the abuse a secret.

Definitions of what behaviors constitute CSA vary among ethnicities and this may also impede reporting. Although CSA is generally construed to involve a misuse of power and coercion of the child for the perpetrator's gain (Jeffries, 2010; National Center for Victims of Crime, 2015), sexual practices in a family's country of origin may include practices which would generally be considered to constitute CSA in the United States. This speaks to the importance of assessing immigration history and acculturation in Muslim American families. Traditional Islamic law, referred to as *Shari'ah* law, while not practiced in the US, may also influence attitudes toward CSA in that the burden of proof rests upon the alleged victim of sexual assault to prove it has occurred (Quraishi, 1999). In some Muslim countries, marriage of underage females, and sexual coercion of male children are practices with long, sometimes secretive, histories, which are sometimes alleged to be justified in terms of cultural traditions and religious tenets (Goldstein, 2015; Rezaeian, 2010). Discussion of these behaviors goes beyond the scope of this chapter but is mentioned here to further suggest that recency of immigration should be assessed by clinicians as this may also influence a family's views about appropriate sexual behaviors and, therefore, reporting of what constitutes CSA. It should also be noted that there are many numerous verses from the *Qur'an* which uphold the rights of children to protection and safety and run counter to allegations that sexual behaviors involving underage children are religiously sanctioned (Dhami & Sheikh, 2000; Frontline, 2010; Jeffries, 2010).

Community Values on Gender and Sexuality

In order to understand why disclosure of CSA may be particularly difficult for members of the Muslim American community, it is important to know some basic tents, particularly the values surrounding gender and sexuality.

Family Structure

As in Orthodox Judaism, family is the most central unit in Islam (Haboush & Alyan, 2013; McAdams-Mahmoud, 2005). Family is viewed as divinely inspired and marriage is at its center.

Traditionally, the Muslim family is extended and usually includes relatives that span across 3 or more generations (Dhami & Sheikh, 2000). Family members of different generations may reside together and elders are afforded considerable respect. Obedience, reputation and respect are valued (Abu Baker & Dwairy, 2003; Ahmed & Amer, 2011). Traditionally fathers are the "head of household" (Ahmed & Amer, 2011; Dhami & Sheikh, 2000; McAdams-Mahmoud, 2005).

Although a central tenet of Islam is to affirm the equality among all human beings regardless of gender, there is a distinct differentiation based on gender regarding the roles a husband and wife carry out within the family (McAdams-Mahmoud, 2005). For instance, the woman's primary duty is to educate and nurture her children while also maintaining connections with the wider family and caring for the home. The man is given the role as "head of the family" and bears responsibility to protect, defend, and support his family. This includes providing financial stability through work.

In comparison to her husband, the woman is largely responsible for her children.

The mother in the Islamic family holds a dual role not only as caregiver but also as educator. Muslim mothers bear a large responsibility to provide knowledge and instill religious beliefs and values within her children (Aljayyousi-Khalil, 2007).

In Islam, marriage is viewed as a religious duty (Dhami & Sheikh, 2000; Haboush & Ansary, n.d.; McAdams-Mahmoud, 2005). Muslims are encouraged to marry within their faith and parents and extended family will often recommend a potential mate within the community. Unmarried females may have a guardian. After puberty, separation of males and females is generally observed for religious and celebratory occasions and physical contact between males and females outside of one's family is discouraged. McAdam-Mahmoud (2005) notes this gender separation is viewed as natural and modest and allows for support to be obtained within the same gender community rather than it being perceived as oppressive.

Modesty and Sexuality

In Islam, views on gender roles, modesty and sexuality are guided by the sacred texts of the *Hadith* and the *Qur'an*. For example, verses in the *Qur'an*

(17:32; 25:68) have been interpreted to mean that sex outside of marriage is a sin which is punishable (Quraishi, 1999). These powerful verses encourage Muslims to not voluntarily engage in such acts, as this activity is not only considered a sin but also a prosecutable criminal offence, known as *zina*. Thus, while sex within marriage is viewed as holy (Dhami & Sheikh, 2000; Gilligan & Akhtar, 2004; Quaraishi, 1999), other types of sexual activity, such as premarital sex and homosexuality are not accepted and constitute potential sources of considerable *sharma* or shame (CAIR 2005a, McAdams-Mahmoud, 2005; Farih et al., 2015; Tabatabaie, 2015).

Both the *Qur'an* and the *Hadith* emphasize the importance of maintaining *haya* (modesty) and *izzat*, meaning honor or respect (Gilligan & Akhtar, 2005). Because of the high-context society of the Islamic culture whereby emphasis is on the group rather than the individual, these attitudes present challenges for the disclosure and discussion of extramarital sex such that, reporting sexual abuse to either family member and/or professionals violates the victim's ability to uphold their modesty. In most cases, a victim is asked to provide extensive details regarding the sexual abuse, which requires the victim to elaborate upon events that the *Qur'an* has deemed to be sinful. CSA by a perpetrator of the same gender may be construed as especially shaming since homosexuality is not permissible (CAIR, 2005a; McAdadms-Mahmoud, 2005) under Islam. Furthermore, it is common practice for hospitals to administer a sexual assault evidence collection kit, which requires the victim to undergo a comprehensive bodily examination. This intrusive procedure leaves no room for modesty as it requires the victim to allow another person to examine their private body parts.

In addition to tarnishing the victim's *izzat*, the mother'*s izzat* may also be in jeopardy. The mother in the Islamic family holds a dual role not only as caregiver but also as educator. Muslim mothers bear a large responsibility to provide knowledge and instill religious beliefs and values within her children (Aljayyousi-Khalil, 2007). In addition, Islamic law declares that children possess the right to protection (Dhami & Sheikh, 2000; Gilligan & Akhtar, 200; Jeffries, 2010). As such, Muslim mothers bear an enormous responsibility to protect their children. If a child is sexually abused, this may raise questions about the mother's ability to monitor and/or educate her children to recognize and avoid dangerous situations. The possibility of societal gossip regarding doubts of the Muslim mother's effectiveness to fulfill her roles may contribute to the family's decision against reporting child sexual abuse.

In sum, regarding *izzat*, the reporting of sexual abuse breaches confidentiality and becomes a public event where the victim's honor is replaced with *sharma*. After reporting sexual abuse, the victim and/or their families position may be compromised and they may face exclusion from the community (Abu Baker & Dwairy, 2003; Gilligan & Akhtar, 2005). This may dramatically affect a child's coping and chances of finding an appropriate partner for marriage (Alyan, 2014), which is so important within observant communities.

Anti-Muslim Bias, *Sharam*, and the Community Legal Process

Following 9/11, Muslim Americans continue to report experiences of discrimination, bias and increased law enforcement surveillance of Muslim communities (Haboush & Alyan, 2013; Pew, 2011). Negative attitudes towards Muslims are prevalent within the post 9/11 American landscape and instances of anti-Muslim bias on communities, work and schools continue to occur. Some Muslim Americans face dual oppression based on both race and religion (McAdams-Mahmoud, 2005; Pew, 2011). In relation to CSA, it is important to consider how possible negative publicity surrounding the sexual abuse of a child in the Islamic community would potentially contribute to the confirmation bias many non-Muslims have towards Muslims. A child, or their parents, may choose not to report abuse as they consider what would be in the best interest for the larger Islamic community. This may be especially challenging in private schools where conflicts around duty to report suspected abuse and allegiance to one's community may be felt. It is also important to consider the culture of today's society, where media plays an integral part in modern day life. Thus, if a child were to report sexual abuse, media attention involving reporters asking intrusive questions in order to gather enough details to write their story could force the child to violate *haya* and provide descriptive information about what happened. In addition, the publication of the story violates *izzat* as a private affair is immediately transformed into a public matter, and therefore a source of *sharma* (Gilligan & Akhtar, 2005). Links to websites that published stories sharing the intimate details of the incident might constitute another such violation. Importantly, the media's overwhelmingly negative portrayal of Muslims has been extensively documented in the literature (Ali et al., 2004; Haboush & Alyan, 2013).

Finally, potential concerns about children being removed from the community and raised in non-Muslim households may also contribute to reluctance to report suspected CSA. Research pertaining to the availability of foster care within the Muslim American community is needed.

Community Legal Process

Historically, observant Muslims resolved issues of injustice through religious avenues, involving consulting with imams and seeking redress through religious courts. Because of *sharma,* observant Muslims may still look to religious leaders for counsel and guidance and prefer to solve issues related to CSA within their community rather than seeking to involve law enforcement. The added scrutiny that many Muslim Americans have encountered post 9/11 may further add to this hesitancy (Haboush & Alyan, 2013). For some Muslims, beliefs about justice and punishment may also be influenced by *Shari'ah* law, which although not recognized with the US legal system, may still exert influence over community values and attitudes, especially in communities where families are more recent immigrants. As noted above, although the *Qur'an* is clear that sex outside marriage is a sin, some verses interpret it to be a prosecutable criminal offence, known as *zina.* Traditionally, victims have needed to provide sufficient evidence of non-consent against their assailant; this might include instances in which the perpetrator confesses to the assault or if there are four eyewitnesses willing to testify (Qurashi, 1999). In some instances, if clear and convincing evidence is not provided to support sexual abuse, the victim may face punishment (see, for example Quraishi, 1999). The strict guidelines that a victim must follow in order to convict their perpetrator of sexual abuse along with the possibility of facing punishment if convincing proof is not provided, contributes to the underreporting of sexual abuse within the Islamic community (Quraishi, 1999). Thus, while *Sharia* law is not adhered to in the US, the belief system which places responsibility upon the victim may still influence the considerations around reporting of CSA and its aftermath in light of the possibility of *sharam* for the family. Assessment of a familie's degree of acculturation is an important variable in this area.

As in Orthodox Judaism, there may be a preference for Islamic counseling and family services to support the child's healing (Haboush & Alyan, 2013; Haboush & Ansary, n.d.). Where possible, collaboration with community leaders such as *imams* and community organizations may be desirable.

FORENSIC CHILD SEX ABUSE INTERVIEWING WITH MUSLIM AMERICAN CHILDREN

Although information on the forensic interviewing of Muslim children and their families is limited, certain considerations discussed with Orthodox Jews might be extended to the Muslim population, in light of overlap with regard to customs, collectivism, and cultural tenets. Similarities include: valuing the importance of family, caution regarding non-Muslim agencies and authorities, modest dress and behavior, religious holidays and observances that are different from traditional American holidays, and a desire to protect one's family and religious community from shame (Ali et al., 2004; Dhami & Shiekh, 2000). The authority granted to fathers may mean the father is the initial point of contact. Research indicates that Muslims often endorse working with someone who is familiar with Islam as important to them, which may facilitate relationship building on the part of the evaluator (Ali et al., 2004; Haboush & Ansary, nd). Thus, building trust may take time. As with Orthodox Jewish families, interviewers should seek knowledge of Muslim customs and religious beliefs and familiarize themselves with specific holidays and observances such as Ramadan. Related to holidays, interviewing on religious fast days might be discussed in advance with parents in light of both the religious and medical/physical considerations.

The importance of modesty in Islam suggests that discussion of sexual matters and CSA by its very nature will be challenging and a potential source of *sharam*. The evaluator is cautioned to remember that many Muslims refrain from openly discussing sexual matters. Girls speaking with female evaluators is more in keeping with modest behavior (Gilligan & Akhtar, 2005). Medical examinations may in and of themselves be a source of shame to both undergo and discuss (CAIR, 2005a). Clinical observations suggest that the conduct of the evaluator in regard to observing modest dress, maintaining an appropriate physical distance from members of the opposite sex, and refraining from physical contact (i.e., handshaking) also apply. These observations are consistent with recommendations in the psychotherapy literature pertaining to culturally competent mental health treatment (Ali et al., 2004; Haboush & Alyan, 2013; McAdams-Mahmoud, 2005).

Interview instructions are also important when conducting a forensic interview with a Muslim child. As with an Orthodox child, Muslim children are taught to respect authority and may need permission to correct the interviewer and not feel they have to answer every question. This will help minimize suggestibility. Direct eye contact with adults may be considered impolite.

The role of adults in supporting children in disclosing extends to family, schools, and mosques, including the *imams* (Abu Baker, 2013; Abu-Baker & Dwairy, 2003; Alyan, 2014; Haboush & Alyan, 2013). Adult support for reporting is needed to counter the strong collectivist emphasis which may be associated with disclosing sexual behavior (Abu-Baker & Dwairy, 2005; Alyan, 2014). The propensity to blame and shame the child may be heightened as the family attempts to retain its place in the community. In school, although teachers are often more likely than other professionals to be aware of suspected abuse (National Center for Victims of Crime, 2015), it is conceivable that loyalty to the community and hesitancy to disclose may be even more strongly felt in private faith-based schools. The current backlash of discrimination against Muslims may further heighten reluctance to engage in any behavior which might cast the community in a negative light (Pashman & McCoppin, 2015; Romo, 2013; Zanbeer, 2014). Empirical research in all of these areas is very much needed, as the support of non-offending adults on the abused child's behalf has been demonstrated to positively relate to their improved coping (Haboush & Alyan, 2013).

There are some notable differences between Muslim Americans and Orthodox Jews apart from their religious beliefs, that may impact the interview, although empirical investigation of these topics remains lacking. Unlike Orthodox Jewish children, many Muslim children attend secular public schools and are, therefore, more exposed to social media such as television, the internet, etc. As a result, they may not have the extent of language barrier that one encounters with many Orthodox Jewish children, as most Muslims speak English quite proficiently (Pew, 2011). These factors may contribute to fewer issues for conducting a culturally competent interview as many Muslim children are also more assimilated and acculturated to American secular society (Pew, 2011). However, extent of acculturation will also be mediated by date of immigration, reasons for immigrating, and current socio-political climate (Ali et al., 2000; Haboush & Ansary, n.d.). Observant Muslims often refrain from listening to loud music, for example, and feel that many aspects of popular media are immodest; thus, extent of acculturation may vary. Further, English language fluency does not in and of itself guarantee a child has the vocabulary to describe body parts and sexual acts, given that children may not receive sex education (Tabatabaie, 2015). Language may also remain a factor in relation to discussion of the *Qur'an* and its guidance on these matters as the *Qur'an* is written in Arabic When interviewing children, some supplementary interviewing aides such as human figure drawings may not be acceptable under Islam which forbids images (CAIR, 2005b). Therefore, the culturally-sensitive evaluator should inquire about the use of drawings prior to conducting the interview.

The aforementioned considerations are intended to raise awareness of cultural issues that may arise in interviewing; these are not intended a professional standards for practice or sources of legal advice.

CONCLUSION

This chapter has focused upon the manner in which Orthodox Judaism and Islam are collectivist cultures in which the practice of religion guides daily life for observant members. While degrees of religiosity will vary among followers, strongly held values will have implications for CSA interviewing. As cases of sexual abuse come to the forefront within these two collectivist communities, professionals who interview children should make every effort to achieve cultural competence (Elwyn et al., 2010; Kuehnle, 2011). Both individual interviewers and agencies need to adapt their protocols and procedures to ensure a sense of trust from community members and to make them feel welcome and respected in light of histories of discrimination (Fontes & Faller, 2007). Members of the Orthodox and Muslim American communities, including religious leaders, need to be educated about the process of forensic investigations in sexual abuse matters; in turn, psychologists need education about different religious cultures. Empirical research on these topics is urged, as the safety of all children is of the upmost importance to uphold.

SUGGESTED RESOURCES

Resources for Orthodox Jews

Bikur Cholim: Bikur Cholim is a program of the Jewish Board of Family and Children's Services, "encompassing a wide range of services that primarily serve the needs of the Orthodox, Ultra-Orthodox, and Hasidic Jewish populations. Bikur Cholim is located throughout the metropolitan New York area as well as in 22 other states and four countries, including Israel. The programs offer clinical psychological services for families in distress, including all types of child abuse, family violence, family dislocation and community violence. They also offer preventive services which focus on strengthening families so they can stay intact through intervention, counseling and treatment. The core mission is to work with families where they are, in order to prevent further fractures in the family structure.

www.bikurcholim.org

My Child Safety Institute: My Child Safety Institute, also known as the Magen Yeladim Child Safety Institute, is a charitable organization founded in 2013 to meet the need for culturally sensitive child abuse prevention materials in the Orthodox Jewish community around the world. The mission of Magen Yeladim Child Safety Institute is to provide a protective safety net for children through preventing the incidence of child abuse, intervening effectively and with cultural sensitivity when abuse occurs; and providing avenues and resources for ongoing support to promote healing for those children and their families. Their services include: education and prevention programs; child safety awareness training; seminars for students; parents and school personnel; liaison with/consultation for institutions, agencies and Jewish Day schools for children of all ages; and community resource research and program development.

www.mychildsafetyinstitute.org

Faith Trust Institute: Faith Trust Institute is a national, multifaith, multicultural training and education organization with global reach working to end sexual abuse and domestic violence. Faith Trust Institute provides multifaith and religion-specific intervention and prevention training, consulting, and educational materials for national, state, and community faith-based and secular organizations in the following areas: Domestic and Sexual Violence; Healthy Teen Relationships; Preventing Teen Dating Violence; Child Abuse; Children and Youth Exposed to Domestic Violence; Healthy Boundaries for Clergy and Spiritual Teachers; Responding to Clergy Misconduct,;and, Trafficking of Persons. They support and advocate for victims of abuse and call perpetrators of abuse to account. They also serve victims and survivors by utilizing education and training as the means to engage in the prevention of sexual and domestic violence, and address religious issues and spiritual needs of victims, survivors, offenders and their communities.

www.faithtrustinstitute.org

Jewish Coalition Against Domestic Violence (JCADA): JCADA addresses the unique needs of Jewish victims and their families in the Greater

Washington Jewish community. Founded in 1999 in response to a pressing need in the Jewish community, JCADA is a non-profit group allied with a host of organizations whose shared mission is to *support* victims of domestic abuse to become empowered and obtain safe environments; e*ducate* community professionals and others about domestic abuse and appropriate responses to it; and p*revent* future generations from suffering domestic abuse by raising awareness. JCADA supports victims of domestic abuse by providing a helpline, crisis counseling, safety planning, support group, and information referral services to all victims of abuse - women, men, teens, and children- in the Greater Washington, D.C. area. JCADA contracts with local clinicians to provide counseling for clients and their families, and has conducted numerous training programs for clinicians to ensure that they are prepared to effectively handle domestic abuse cases.

www.jcada.org

Project SARAH: Project S.A.R.A.H. (Stop Abusive Relationships At Home) is a program that works to overcome cultural, legal and religious barriers confronting victims of domestic violence and sexual abuse. They provide services and resources for Jewish victims of domestic violence and sexual abuse throughout the state of New Jersey and is based at the Jewish Family Service of Clifton/Passaic. They are funded by the N.J. Department of Law & Public Safety, U.S. Department of Justice's Office of Violence Against Women, N.J. Department of Children and Families, Jewish Family Service & Children's Center of Clifton-Passaic and private donations and foundations. No one is turned away due to race, gender or financial difficulties. They serve as a bridge between victims of abuse in the Orthodox community and the support systems and resources available to them. They work closely with rabbis and *rebbetzins, kallah* teachers and *mikvah* attendants, camp directors and school administrators, parents and the general public to help keep the community safe for everyone. Their clinical staff provides therapeutic interventions that enable victims to process the trauma they experienced and restore them toward fully functional and productive lives. They connect victims and survivors with a broad array of services including pro bono legal consultations, evaluations, individual and group therapy, psychiatric services, as well as emotional, financial and vocational support. They also offer abuse prevention programs for camps, schools and synagogues and teach safety skills to thousands of Jewish day school children, parents and teachers.

www.jfsclinton.org/projectsarah

Resources for Muslim Americans

Project Sakinah: This project is dedicated to addressing to addressing domestic violence in Muslim communities. "Take Action" and "Resources and Tools" tabs offer advice and resources for victims/families at: http://projectsakinah.org/which is a resource Older People Surviving Child Sexual Abuse

Importantly, this site also has links to Pandora's Project, which has support and resources for survivors of rape and sexual abuse:

http://www.pandys.org/

Islamic Circle of North America: Resources for obtaining family counseling and other mental health services. Includes: Muslim Family Services:

http://muslimfamilyservices.org/site2/

REFERENCES

Abney, V. D. (2002). Cultural Competency in the Field of Child Maltreatment. In: J. E. Myers (Ed.), *The APSAC handbook on child maltreatment* (pp. 477-486). Thousand Oaks: Sage Publications.

Abu-Baker, K. (2013). Arab parents' reactions to child sexual abuse: A review of clinical records. *Journal of Child Sexual Abuse*, 22, 52-71.

Abu Baker, K. and Dwairy, M. (2003). Cultural norms versus state law in treating incest: A suggested model for Arab families. *Child Abuse and Neglect*, 27, 109-123.

Ahmed, S. and Amer, M. M. (2011). *Counseling Muslims: Handbook of mental health issues and interventions.* New York: Routledge.

Ali, S. R., Liu, W. M. and Humedian, M. (2004). Islam 101: Understanding the religion and therapy implications. *Professional Psychology*, 35, 635-642.

Aljayyousi-Khalil, G. (2007). Mother-daughter relationships within a Muslim community and the influence on American Muslim adolescent daughters' health behavior (Unpublished doctoral dissertation). Kansas State University, Manhattan, Kansas.

Alyan, H. N. (2014). *Experiences of Arab immigrant and Arab-American survivors of sexual violence: An exploratory study* (Unpublished doctoral dissertation). GSAPP, Rutgers University, Piscataway, NJ.

American Psychological Association. (2015). Statement of Board of Directors--Living in a World of Diverse Religions. Retrieved from: http://www.apa.org /news/press/op-ed/diverse-religions.

American Psychological Association (2010). Ethical Principles of Psychologists and Code of Conduct (with 2010 Amendments). Retrieved from http://www.apa.org/ethics/code/principles.pdf.

Ayoub, C. and Kinscherff, R. (2006). Forensic Assessment of Parenting in Child Abuse and Neglect Cases. In: S. N. Sparta and G. P. Koocher (Eds.), *Forensic mental health assessment of children and adolescents* (pp. 330-341). Oxford: Oxford University Press.

Azam, H. (2013). Rape as a variant of fornication (Zinā) in Islamic Law: An examination of the early legal reports. *Journal of Law and Religion*, 28, 441-466.

Biale, R. (1995). Women and Jewish law: The essential texts, their history, and their relevance *for today*. New York: Schocken Books.

Caudill, O. B. (2006). Avoiding Malpractice in Child Forensic Assessment. In: S. N. Sparta and G. P. Koocher (Eds.), *Forensic mental health assessment of children and adolescents* (pp. 74-87). Oxford: Oxford University Press.

Council on American-Islamic Relations (CAIR). (2005a). A healthcare provider's guide to Islamic religious practices. Washington, DC: CAIR.

Council on American-Islamic Relations (CAIR). (2005b). An educator's guide to Islamic religious principles. Washington, DC: CAIR.

Dhami, S. and Sheikh, A. (2000). The Muslim family: predicament and promise. *Western Journal of Medicine*, 173(5), 352-356.

Elwyn, T. S., Tseng, W. S. and Matthews, D. (2010). Cultural Competence in Child and Adolescent Forensic Mental Health. In: E. P. Benedek, P. Ash and C. L. Scott (Eds.), *Principles and practice of child and adolescent forensic mental health* (pp. 91-106). Washington, DC: American Psychiatric Pub.

Faller, K. C. and Fontes, L. A. (2007). Conducting Culturally Competent Sexual Abuse Interviews with Children. In: *Interviewing children about sexual abuse: Controversies and best practice* (pp. 164-174). Oxford: Oxford University Press.

Faller, K. C. (2007). Interviewing children about sexual abuse: Controversies and best practice. Oxford: Oxford University Press.

Farih, M., Freeth, D., Khan, K. and Meads, C. (2015). Sexual and reproductive health knowledge and information-seeking behavior among middle eastern female university students: A systematic review. *International Journal of Sexual Health*, doi: 10.1080/19317611.2015.1023961.

Featherman, J. M. (1995). Jews and Sexual Child Abuse. In: L. A. Fontes (Ed.), *Sexual abuse in nine North American cultures: Treatment and prevention* (pp. 128-155). Thousand Oaks, CA: Sage Publications.

Fontes, L. A. (2005). Child abuse and culture: Working with diverse families. New York: Guilford Press.

Frontline: The dancing boys of Afghanistan (2010). *Frontline*. Retrieved from: http://www.pbs.org/wgbh/pages/frontline/dancingboys/view/.

Gilligan, P. and Akhtar, S. (2005). Cultural barriers to the disclosure of child sexual abuse in Asian communities: Listening to what women say. *British Journal of Social Work, 36*, 1361-1377. doi:10.1093/bjsw/bch309.

Goldstein, A. (Sept. 20, 2015). US Soldiers told to ignore sexual abuse of boys by Afghan Allies. *The New York Times*. Retrieved from: http://www.nytimes.com/2015/09/21/world/asia/us-soldiers-told-to-ignore-afghan-allies-abuse-of-boys.html?_r=0.

Haboush, K. L. and Ansary, N. (Manuscript in preparation). Muslim couples and families. In: S. Kelly (Ed.), *Issues in couple and family psychology: Across socioeconomics, ethnicities, and sexualities* (pp. xx-xx). NewYork: Praeger.

Haboush, K. L. and Alyan, H. (2013). "Who Can You Tell?": Features of Arab culture that influence conceptualization and treatment of childhood sexual abuse. *Journal of Child Sexual Abuse, 22*, 499-518.

Hershkowitz, I., Orbach, Y., Sternberg, K. J., Pipe, M. E., Lamb, M. E. and Horowitz, D. (2007). Suspected Victims of Abuse who do Not Make Allegations. In: M. Pipe (Ed.), *Child sexual abuse: Disclosure, delay, and denial* (pp. 97-113). Mahwah, NJ: Lawrence Erlbaum Associates.

Jeffries, L. (2010). *Protecting children from sexual abuse-II*. Retrieved from http://www.islamweb.net/emainpage/printarticle.php?id=156876&lang=E.

Koocher, G. P. (2006). Ethical Issues in Forensic Assessment of Children and Adolescents. In: S. N. Sparta ad G. P. Koocher (Eds.), *Forensic mental health assessment of children and adolescents* (pp. 46-63). Oxford: Oxford University Press.

Kuehnle, K. and Connell, M. (2009). *The evaluation of child sexual abuse allegations: A comprehensive guide to assessment and testimony*. Hoboken, NJ: Wiley.

Kuehnle, K. and Sparta, S. (2006). Assessing Child Sexual Abuse Allegations in a Legal Context. In: S. N. Sparta and G. P. Koocher (Eds.), *Forensic mental health assessment of children and adolescents* (pp. 129-148). Oxford: Oxford University Press.

Kuehnle, K. (1996). *Assessing allegations of child sexual abuse*. Sarasota, FL: Professional Resource Press.

Kuehnle, K. (2011). *Assessing allegations of child sexual abuse*. Sarasota, FL: Professional Resource Press.

Lamb, M. E., Hershkowitz, I., Orbach, Y. and Esplin, P. W. (2008). *Tell me what happened: Structured investigative interviews of child victims and witnesses*. Chichester, England: Wiley-Blackwell.

Lesher, M. (2014). Sexual abuse, shonda and concealment in Orthodox Jewish communities. Jefferson, North Carolina: MacFarland and Company Inc. Publishers.

Lightman, E. and Shor, R. (2002). Askanim: Informal helpers and cultural brokers as a bridge to secular helpers for the Ultra-Orthodox Jewish communities of Israel and Canada. *Families in Society: The Journal of Contemporary Social Services*, 83(3), 315-324. doi:10.1606/1044-3894.26.

McAdams-Mahmoud, V. (2005). African American Muslim families. In: M. McGoldrick, J. Giordano and N. Garcia-Preto (Eds.), *Ethnicity and Family Therapy* (3rd ed., pp. 138-150). New York: The Guilford Press.

Merrell, K. W., Ervin, R. A. and Gimpel, G. P. (2012). *School psychology for the 21st century: Foundations and practices* (2nd ed.). New York: The Guilford Press.

Meyers, J. E., Berliner, L., Briere, J., Hendrix, C. T., Jenny, C. and Reid, T. A. (Eds.). (2002). *The APSAC handbook on child maltreatment* (2nd ed.). Thousand Oaks, CA: Sage Publications.

National Center for Victims of Crime. (2015). Reporting on child sexual abuse. Retrieved from: https://www.victimsofcrime.org/media/reporting-on-child-sexual-abuse/child-sexual-abuse-statistics.

Neustein, A. (2009). *Tempest in the temple: Jewish communities and child sex scandals*. Waltham, MA: Brandeis University Press.

Newlin, C., Steele, L. C., Chamberlin, A., Anderson, J., Kenniston, J., Russell, A. and Vaughn-Eden, V. (2015, September). *Ojjdp.gov* (United States, Department of Justice, Office of Juvenile Justice and Deliquency Prevention).

Orbach, Y., Shiloach, H. and Lamb, M. E. (2007). Reluctant Disclosures of Child Sexual Abuse. In: M. Pipe (Ed.), *Child sexual abuse: Disclosure, delay, and denial* (pp. 115-134). Mahwah, NJ: Lawrence Erlbaum Associates.

Paradis, C. M., Friedman, S., Hatch, M. L. and Ackerman, R. (1996). Cognitive behavioral treatment of anxiety disorders in Orthodox Jews.

Cognitive and Behavioral Practice, 3 (2), 271-288. doi:10.1016/s1077-7229(96)80018-6.

Pashman, M. B. and McCoppin, R. (2015). South Asian community shocked at sexual assault against Elgin imam. Retrieved from http://www.chicago tribune.com/news/local/breaking/chi-chicago-muslim-religious-leader.

Pence, D. (2011). *The APSAC handbook on child maltreatment* (pp. 325-375) (J. E. Myers, Ed.). Los Angeles: SAGE.

Pew Research Center. (2011). Muslim Americans. Retrieved from http://www.pewresearchcenter.org.

Pew Research Center. (2015a). A portrait of American Orthodox Jews. Retrieved from: http://www.pewresearchcenter.org.

Pew Research Center. (2015b). America's changing religious landscape. Retrieved from: http://www.pewresearchcenter.org.

Pew Research Center. (2015c). The future of the world religions: Population growth projections, 2010-2050.

Pipe, M., Lamb, M. E., Orbach, Y. and Cederborg, A. (Eds.). (2007). *Child sexual abuse: Disclosure, delay, and denial.* Mahwah, NJ: Lawrence Erlbaum Associates.

Pipe, M. and Salmon, K. (2009). Dolls, Drawings, Body Diagrams, and Other Props. In: K. Kuehnle and M. Connell (Eds.), *The evaluation of child sexual abuse allegations: A comprehensive guide to assessment and testimony* (pp. 365-395). Hoboken, NJ: Wiley.

Poole, D. A. and Lamb, M. E. (1998). *Investigative interviews of children: A guide for helping professionals.* Washington, DC: American Psychological Association.

Quraishi, A. (1999). Her honour: An Islamic critique of the rape provisions in Pakistan's ordinance on zina. *Islamic Studies*, 38, 403-431.

Rezaeian, M. (2010). Suicide among young Middle Eastern Muslim females. *Crisis: The Journal of Crisis Intervention and Suicide Prevention*, 31, 36-42.

Romo, J. (2013). Responsibilities of faith-based groups regarding child sexual abuse. *Family and Intimate Partner Violence Quarterly* 6, 276-288.

Saywitz, K. J. (2002). Interviewing Children. In: J. E. Myers (Ed.), *The APSAC handbook on child maltreatment* (pp. 337-360). Thousand Oaks: Sage Publications.

Schnall, E. (2006). Multicultural Counseling and the Orthodox Jew. *Journal of Counseling and Development*, 84(3), 276-282. doi:10.1002/j.1556-6678.2006.tb00406.x.

Silverman, S. (2014). *Shalomtaskforce.org* (United States, Department of Health and Human Services, National Resource Center for Healthy Marriage and Families).

Sublette, E. and Trappler, B. (2000). Cultural Sensitivity Training in Mental Health: Treatment of Orthodox Jewish Psychiatric Inpatients. *International Journal of Social Psychiatry*, 46(2), 122-134. doi:10.1177/002076400004600205.

Tabatabaie, A. (2015.) Childhood and adolescent sexuality, Islam, and problematic of sex education: A call for re-examination. *Sex Education*, 15, 3, 276-288, DOI: 10.1080/14681811.2015.1005836.

Tishelman, A. C., Newton, A. W., Denton, J. E. and Vandeven, A. M. (2006). Child Physical Abuse and Neglect: Medical and Other Considerations in Forensic Psychological Assessment. In: S. N. Sparta and G. P. Koocher (Eds.), *Forensic mental health assessment of children and adolescents* (pp. 175-189). Oxford: Oxford University Press.

Weinrach, S. G. (2002). The Counseling Profession's Relationship to Jews and the Issues That Concern Them: More Than a Case of Selective Awareness. *Journal of Counseling and Development,* 80(3), 300-314. doi:10.1002/j.1556-6678.2002.tb00195.x.

Zaneer, Z. (2014). Sexually abused when they were kids (stories). Retrieved from: http://www.onislam.net/english/family/your-society/torn-apart-/461583 -sexually-abused.

BIOGRAPHICAL SKETCHES

Name: **Karen L. Haboush, PsyD**
Affiliation:
1. Clinical Associate Professor and School Psychology Internship Coordinator, GSAPP, Rutgers University
2. Clinical Associate Professor, Department of Psychiatry, Robert Wood Johnson Medical School, New Brunswick, New Jersey
3. Licensed Psychologist in Independent Practice, Highland Park, NJ 08904

Address:

1) GSAPP, Rutgers University, 152 Frelinghuysen Road, Piscataway, NJ 08854,

2) Department of Psychiatry, Robert Wood Johnson Medical School, New Brunswick, New Jersey
3) Independent Practice: Highland Park, NJ 08904

Research and Professional Experience:
Karen L. Haboush is a Core Faculty member in the APA/NASP approved school psychology program. She received her PsyD from Rutgers university in 1989. Her primary clinical and scholarly interests include: supervision and professional development of school psychologists, comprehensive school-based mental health programs for at-risk and urban youth, integration of attachment theory and psychodynamic theories with school psychology practice, international school psychology, play therapy, treatment of trauma and child sexual abuse, personality assessment, gender and ethnicity. She has published journal articles and book chapters on clinical supervision, trauma, psychological assessment, and culturally-competent psychological practice with Middle Eastern children and families. As the School Psychology Internship and Practicum Coordinator, she develops school psychology practicum sites and doctoral internship sites for the Rutgers School Psychology Internship Consortium. She maintains a full time private practice in Highland Park, New Jersey working with children and providing school consultation. She draws on her clinical practice as well as her previous supervisory positions in school-based mental health programs when teaching and supervising to model the integration of theory and practice. Karen is active in presenting at state and international professional groups aimed at promoting school psychology practice with traumatized and underserved children.

Professional Appointments:
1) Clinical Associate Professor and School Psychology Internship Coordinator, GSAPP, RU
2) Clinical Associate Professor, Department of Psychiatry, Robert Wood Johnson Medical School, New Brunswick, New Jersey

Honors:
2009 Rutgers University PTL Instructors Award.

Publications Last 3 Years:
Haboush, K. L. andAnsary, N. (Manuscript in preparation). Muslim couples and families. In: Shalonda Kelly (Ed.), *Issues in couple and family*

psychology: Across socioeconomics, ethnicities, and sexualities (pp. xx-xx). NewYork: Praeger.

Haboush, K. L., Meltzer, A., Wang, R. and Hamsho, N. (Manuscript in preparation). Cultural competence and child interviewing: Understanding religious factors in child sex abuse interviewing. In: … (Ed.) *Sexual abuse: Intervention, coping strategies, and psychological impact,* Nova Science Publishers: Haupage, NY.

Haboush, K. L., Mosdell, C., Polyeff, L. and Lefkowitz. (Manuscript in preparation). Graduate school as a holding environment: The role of attachment theory in school psychology training programs.

Haboush, K. L. and Alyan, H. (2015). School psychology: Enhancing school climate and school connectedness. In: M. M. Amer and G. H. Awad (Eds.), *Handbook of Arab American psychology.* New York: Routledge.

Haboush, K. L. and Barakat, N. (2014). Education and employment among Arab Americans: Pathways to individual identity and community resilience. In: Sylvia C. Nassar-McMillan, Kristine J. Ajrouch and Julie Hakim-Larson (Eds.), *Biopsychosocial perspectives on Arab Americans: Culture, development, and health identity and community resilience* (pp. 229-255). New York: Springer Publishing.

Haboush, K. L. and Alyan, H. (2013). "Who Can You Tell?": Features of Arab culture that influence conceptualization and treatment of childhood sexual abuse. *Journal of Child Sexual Abuse*, 22, 499-518.

Haboush, K. L. (2010). Interviews with culture-specific experts: Middle Eastern clients. In: A. M. Pomerantz (Ed.), *Student study site for Clinical psychology: Science, practice, and culture.* 2nd ed. (pp. 26-29). http://www.sagepub.com/pomerantz2e/study/resources.htm.

Haboush, K. L. (2010). Middle Eastern clients. In: A. M. Pomerantz (Ed.), *Clinical psychology: Science, practice, and culture.* 2nd ed. (pp. 70-71). New York: Sage.

Name: **Anne H. Meltzer, PsyD**
Affiliation: Independent Practice
Education: Psy.D. Yeshiva University
MA Tufts University
BA Clark University
Address: 15 Leatherstocking Lane, Scarsdale, New York 10583

Research and Professional Experience:

Anne Meltzer is a leading clinical expert in the forensic evaluation of alleged child sexual abuse victims and maintains a private practice in both New York City and Westchester County, New York. She has evaluated over 800 children and testified on approximately 400 occasions as an expert witness in both Family and Criminal Courts. She works as a consultant to Child Protective Agencies throughout the greater New York City area, as well as prosecuting attorneys, defense attorneys, law guardians for the children, and health care professionals. She has lectured widely in the area of forensic interviewing techniques and expert witness issues to members of the legal, medical, and mental health professions. She is a licensed psychologist in the state of New York as well as a certified teacher and school psychologist in the states of New York and Massachusetts.

Name: Rachel Wang
Affiliation: Rutgers University
Education: Colgate University,
BA/Rutgers University, Doctoral Candidate
Address: 215 Park Avenue Apt 6 Hoboken, NJ 07030

Researchand Professional Experience:
Brady Foundation Collaborative Coaching Project, Rutgers University 2015
Research Assistant Scholarship, Rutgers University 2014-2015

Honors: Alpha Kappa Delta Sociology Honors Society 2010

Name: Narmene Hamsho
Affiliation: Syracuse University
Education: B.A
Address: 502 Walnut Avenue Syracuse, NY 13210

Research and Professional Experience:
Narmene Hamsho is a doctoral student currently a student clinician providing treatment to individuals with varying diagnoses. In addition, she is a graduate intern at a local refugee center and provides emotional/behavioral and academic support to refugee children between the ages of 4 and 7. Narmene

also recently served as an advocate for a crisis center where she assisted victims of sexual assault and/or family violence in securing the necessary information, services, and follow-up care that were appropriate for each individual.

Narmene's research experience complements her professional experience, with the goal of identifying important factors impacting treatment delivery in order to enhance the effectiveness of interventions. For instance, current projects include the following goals: examining the influence of parental ADHD on the parenting behaviors of parents of adolescents in order to understand how this might affect interventions targeting behavioral parent training; examine childhood predictors of adolescent written expression in 22q11.2 Deletion Syndrome in order to offer some guidance for how to best consider intervention efforts to improve written expression skills in adolescents with this genetic syndrome; and determining the relationship between writing performance and classroom behaviors in order to understand how behavior might impact interventions targeting typically developing third graders.

Professional Appointments: Doctoral Student Candidate

Honors:

- Graduate Student Organization (GSO) outreach committee member
- Psychology Action Committee (PAC) Secretary (Fall 2014-Spring 2015), Syracuse University
- Graduate Tuition Scholarship (2014-present), Syracuse University
- Psi Chi (2013-present), International honor society in psychology

Psychology Honors Program (2013-present), University at Buffalo.

In: Sexual Abuse   ISBN: 978-1-63484-509-0
Editor: Olivia Parsons   © 2016 Nova Science Publishers, Inc.

Chapter 4

SEXUAL ABUSE AND THE PSYCHOLOGICAL IMPACT ON CHILDREN: A REVIEW OF THE LITERATURE

Allison N. Sinanan, PhD, MSW
Stockton University, Galloway, NJ, US

ABSTRACT

Research to date has indicated that the psychological effects of childhood sexual abuse are multiple, extensive, and characterized by a boundless amount of variability. Various factors such as frequency and duration of abuse, type of sexual contact, the degree of relationship between the perpetrator and victim will result in differential psychological effects. Experts differ regarding the psychological impact of child sexual abuse, with opinions ranging from the widely-held belief that the impact is vast and irreversible to the controversial perspective that it has very little psychological impact on the child (Gagnon, 1965; La Barbera, Martin, & Dozier, 1980; Mannarino & Cohen, 1986). Many of the early studies reporting minimal impact from child sexual abuse relied more upon anecdotal evidence, calling into question the reliability of their findings. Other studies have been retrospective. Victims of child sexual abuse present with a diverse variety of symptoms rather than a specific abuse profile, and symptom levels for sexually abused children. This chapter will present potential cognitive mediators associated with the psychological impact of childhood sexual abuse by reviewing past and current literature on the effects of this type of abuse.

INTRODUCTION

Research to date has indicated that the psychological effects of childhood sexual abuse are multiple, extensive, and characterized by a boundless amount of variability. Various factors such as frequency and duration of abuse, type of sexual contact, the degree of relationship between the perpetrator and victim will result in differential psychological effects. Experts differ regarding the psychological impact of child sexual abuse, with opinions ranging from the widely-held belief that the impact is vast and irreversible to the controversial perspective that it has very little psychological impact on the child (Gagnon, 1965; La Barbera, Martin, & Dozier, 1980; Mannarino & Cohen, 1986. Children who face sexual abuse not only endure horrific trauma, but also are likely to experience negative symptomatology as a result of this horrific ordeal.

Many of the early studies reporting minimal impact from child sexual abuse relied more upon anecdotal evidence, calling into question the reliability of their findings. Other studies have been retrospective. Victims of child sexual abuse present with a diverse variety of symptoms rather than a specific abuse profile, and symptom levels for sexually abused children. This chapter will present potential cognitive mediators associated with the psychological impact of childhood sexual abuse by reviewing past and current literature on the effects of this type of abuse.

WHAT IS CHILD SEXUAL ABUSE?

Sexual abuse can be hard to define because of the many different forms it can take on, the different levels of frequency, the variation of circumstances it can occur within, and the different relationships that it may be associated with. Maltz (2002) gives the following definition: "sexual abuse occurs whenever one person dominates and exploits another by means of sexual activity or suggestion" (Maltz, 2001a, as cited in Maltz, 2002, p. 321). Ratican (1992) defines childhood sexual abuse as: any sexual act, overt or covert, between a child and an adult (or older child, where the younger child's participation is obtained through seduction or coercion). Irrespective of how childhood sexual abuse is defined it generally has significant negative and pervasive psychological impact on its victims, the impact of childhood sexual abuse varies from person to person and from case to case.

Child sexual abuse (CSA) plagues the lives of millions of children worldwide and has the potential to adversely impact the victim. The rates of child sexual abuse are astounding and provide insight into the seriousness of this epidemic. In 2012, approximately 90,000 children in the United States were reported to child protective services for suspected child sexual abuse. The actual number is likely to be higher because these numbers reflect only children whose cases are investigated by child protective services. It is estimated that 1 in 4 girls and 1 in 6 boys will have experienced an episode of sexual abuse while younger than 18 years. The numbers of boys affected may be falsely low because of reporting techniques (US Department of Health and Human Services, Administration for Children and Families, 2012). Retrospective surveys reveal considerable variation in the prevalence rates for child sexual abuse. Bolen (2001) estimated the prevalence of child sexual abuse ranging from 12% to 18% for females and from 2% to 12% for males. According to Vogeltanz (1999) methodological factors such as sampling methods, methods of data collection, response rates, definition of child sexual abuse, and types of questions used to assess the abuse many contribute to the variability in the prevalence rates.

With such a high percentage of people having experienced childhood sexual abuse, it is likely that many people seeking therapy will have histories that include sexual abuse. It is imperative that counselors are aware of and familiar with the symptoms and long-term effects associated with childhood sexual abuse to help gain a deeper understanding of what is needed in counseling. Research to date has indicated that the psychological effects of childhood sexual abuse are multiple, extensive, and characterized by a boundless amount of variability. Various factors such as frequency and duration of abuse, type of sexual contact, the degree of relationship between the perpetrator and victim will result in differential psychological effects.

One study aimed at arriving at an estimate of the worldwide prevalence of CSA by conducting a meta-analysis of 217 publications published between 1980 and 2008, including 331 independent samples giving a total of 9,911,748 participants (Stoltenborgh, van IJzendoorn, Euser, & Bakermans-Kranenburg, 2011). After conducting exhaustive research, the researchers concluded that the worldwide prevalence of CSA for females is between 164/1,000 (16.4%) and 197/1,000 (19.7%) and for males is between 66/1,000 (6.6%) and 88/1,000 (8.8%) (Stoltenborgh et al., 2011). It must be noted that these numbers, however, included only reported cases of sexual abuse and do not take into account the myriad of unreported sexual abuse cases. The actual prevalence of child sexual abuse is likely higher than previously stated, as these numbers are based on self-report and many people are hesitant to reveal information regarding CSA. Underreporting of CSA leads us to believe that the numbers of reported cases of CSA in both men and women are less than the actual number of sexual abuse cases.

CHILDHOOD SEXUAL ABUSE DEFINITION

There is no universal definition of child sexual abuse; however, government and state agencies have produced definitions to aid in the prosecution of offenders and provide guidelines for those who are mandated to report child sexual abuse. The Child Abuse and Treatment Act (CAPTA) defines sexual abuse as: the employment, use, persuasion, inducement, enticement, or coercion of any child to engage in, or assist any other person to engage in, any sexually explicit conduct or simulation of such conduct for the purpose of producing a visual depiction of such conduct; or the rape, and in cases of caretaker or inter-familial relationships, statutory rape, molestation, prostitution, or other form of sexual exploitation of children, or incest with children (Child Welfare Information Gateway, 2011, p. 2). Physical symptoms such as irritable bowel syndrome, chronic fatigue, non-epileptic seizures, and fibromyalgia are common symptoms linked to survivors of childhood sexual abuse (Arias, 2004; Maniglio, 2009). Although not all children who have been the victim of childhood sexual abuse develop mental health or medical problems, empirical research highly suggest heightened levels of dysfunction among the victims.

PSYCHOLOGICAL EFFECTS AND TRAUMA

Childhood sexual trauma can have a profoundly devastating effect upon an individual. Some people appear to be relatively asymptomatic, while others can be impacted greatly. Sexual trauma can impact many of the normal developmental processes of childhood; typically exhibited by emotional or behavioral features that show distress. According to the literature, child sexual abuse is a risk factor for the development of an array of intra and interpersonal difficulties, including depression, anxiety, post-traumatic stress, dissociation, personality and eating disorders, and dyadic distress (Finkelhor & Browne, 1985; DiLillo, 2001; Neumann, Houskamp, Pollock, & Briere, 1996).

Childhood sexual abuse has been correlated with higher levels of depression, guilt, shame, self-blame, eating disorders, somatic concerns, anxiety, dissociative patterns, repression, denial, sexual problems, relationship problems and trauma. The psychological effects of child sexual abuse often occur irrespective of the particular extent of trauma the child experienced during the abuse. With respect to trauma, the American Psychiatric Association's *Diagnostic and Statistical Manual, Fifth Edition (DSM-5)*, classify the trigger to Post Traumatic Stress Disorder (PTSD) as exposure to actual or threatened death, serious injury or sexual violation. The DSM-V offers four distinct diagnostic clusters described as: re-experiencing, avoidance, negative cognitions and mood, and arousal. The exposure must result from one or more of the following scenarios in which the individual: directly experiences the traumatic event; witnesses the traumatic event in person; learns that the traumatic event occurred to a close family member or close friend (with the actual or threatened death being either violent or accidental); or experiences first-hand repeated or extreme exposure to aversive details of the traumatic event (not through media, pictures, television or movies unless work-related). It must be noted that there are differences in criteria PTSD among adults and children; the *DSM–5* lists the distinction between the two populations, but makes the differentiation for criteria for children less than 6 years of age. The *DSM-5* lists the following diagnostic criteria for PTSD in adults, adolescents, and children older than 6 years:

- Exposure to actual or threatened death, serious injury, or sexual violation
- Presence of 1 or more specified intrusion symptoms in association with the traumatic event(s)
- Persistent avoidance of stimuli associated with the traumatic event(s)
- Negative alterations in cognitions and mood associated with the traumatic event(s)
- Marked alterations in arousal and reactivity associated with the traumatic events(s)
- Duration of the disturbance exceeding 1 month
- Clinically significant distress or impairment in important areas of functioning
- Inability to attribute the disturbance to the physiologic effects of a substance or another medical condition

DSM-5 criteria for PTSD in children aged 6 years or younger are as follows:

- Exposure to actual or threatened death, serious injury, or sexual violation
- Presence of 1 or more specified intrusion symptoms in association with the traumatic event(s)
- Symptoms indicating either persistent avoidance of stimuli associated with the traumatic event(s) or negative alterations in cognitions and mood associated with the event(s)
- Marked alterations in arousal and reactivity associated with the traumatic events(s)
- Duration of the disturbance exceeding 1 month
- Clinically significant distress or impairment in relationships with parents, siblings, peers, or other caregivers or in school behavior
- Inability to attribute the disturbance to the physiologic effects of a substance or another medical condition

There are many contributing factors that determine the extent of the negative impact of childhood sexual trauma (Finkelhor & Browne, 1985). Children are more likely to suffer to a greater extent if the perpetrator is a close relative such as a father as opposed to a neighbor. Children who were sexually abused during earlier stages of development have fewer resources which would allow them to cope and may suffer more adverse consequences (Kendall-Tackett, Williams & Finkelhor, 1993; Knutson, 1995). Sexual abuse may occur as a single incident or it may have continued over a number of months or years.

Even though a child may not be truly cognizant of what is sexually occurring, he/she can still unfortunately experience the negative psychological consequences. The common psychological effects include: depression, anxiety, internal somatic complaints, and thought problems (Gibb, 2002, Garber & Flynn, 2001; Maltz, 2002). Specifically, with respect to depression, research has suggested that a history of child sexual abuse is associated with a negative cognitive style (i.e., internal, global, and stable) in adulthood which has been suggested as a risk factor in the development of depression (Garber & Flynn, 2001; Hankin, Abramson, & Siler, 2001; Stein, Walker, Anderson, Geri; Hazen & Andrea, 1996). Depression has been found to be the most common long-term symptom among survivors.

For survivors of childhood sexual abuse, feelings of confusion, disorientation, nightmares, flashbacks, and difficulty experiencing feelings can occur. Dissociation is also a symptom of this abuse. Some survivors of child sexual abuse may dissociate to protect themselves from experiencing the sexual abuse and continue to use this coping mechanism when they feel unsafe or threatened as adults (King, Tonge, & Mullen, 2000).

It is essential to note that although research has shown there to be significant long-term effect variables and childhood sexual abuse, each victim's symptoms and experiences will not be the same. Although it is often viewed as a traumatic experience, there is no single symptom among all survivors and it is imperative for clinicians to focus on the individual needs of the client. Mental health professionals must be careful not to treat each survivor of abuse as having the same symptomology.

Victims of child sexual abuse attempt numerous efforts to psychologically escape from the abuse (e.g., avoidance, attempts at memory repression, distraction, addictive behaviors) and cognitive efforts at coping (e.g., cognitive reappraisal, reframing, minimization, and working through the abuse, among others). There are many contributing factors that determine the extent of the negative impact of childhood sexual trauma (Finkelhor & Browne, 1985). Children are more likely to suffer to a greater extent if the perpetrator is a close relative such as a father as opposed to a neighbor. Children who were sexually abused during earlier stages of development have fewer resources which would allow them to cope and may suffer more adverse consequences.

The psychological effects of child sexual abuse often occur irrespective of the particular extent of trauma the child experienced during the abuse. Sexual abuse may occur as a single incident or it may have continued over a number of months or years. Sexual violation can also range from inappropriate comments to penetration. The wounds incurred from as a result of childhood sexual trauma are often compounded by other forms of stress or trauma. Even though a child may not be truly cognizant of what is sexually occurring or the wrong doing that he/she is a victim of, they can still unfortunately experience the negative psychological consequences. The common psychological effects include: depression, anxiety, internal somatic complaints, and thought problems. Specifically, with respect to depression, research has suggested that a history of child sexual abuse is associated with a negative cognitive style (i.e., internal, global, and stable) in adulthood which has been suggested as a risk factor in the development of depression (Gibb, 2002, Garber & Flynn, 2001; Hankin, Abramson, & Siler, 2001; Stein, Walker, Anderson, Geri; Hazen & Andrea, 1996).

SYSTEMS THEORY AND BETRAYAL

An underlying concept in general systems theory is that of boundaries. A boundary binds together the components that make up the system, protects them from environmental stresses, and controls entry of resources and information (Miller, 1978). When a child is sexually abused, an obvious boundary of their sexual and physical health has been broken by the perpetrator. Child sexual abuse, according to the tenets of general systems theory, represents a flaw in the family system's capability to uphold correct spatial relationships. Sexual abuse of children is, therefore, an improper crossing of boundaries. This betrayal of broken boundaries of trust, among other factors, affects the child victim psychologically in a variety of ways. Incest, the ultimate break of trust of boundaries greatly affects the coping strategies of the child victim.

Since child sexual abuse occurs when identity and cognitive schemas are developing, the abuse may become a part of the victim's internal representations of the self and self in relation to others (Fergusson, Horwood, & Lynskey, 1996; Toth, Maughan, Manly, Spagnola, & Cicchetti, 2002). Consequently, because incest occurs during formative years, the abuse may develop as a "norm" for the child. This can lead to an unfortunate feeling that complicates a child's perspective on the abuse may be the case that a child may have extreme guilt because he or she feels he or she has done something wrong by being a part of the abuse and does not possess the mental capacity to understand that he or she is a victim. Hence, the victim might experience irritability when he or she does not know how to cope with the confusion or possess the ability to talk about the abuse to others. Children do not have the same resources as adults. They are completely dependent upon the adults entrusted to care for them, and that can leave them extremely vulnerable. Children may not understand that others act independently of them and that their motivations are often less than pure. That's why they often feel responsible for what has happened to them.

Children, specifically younger children, depend exclusively on parents/caregivers for survival and protection—both physical and emotional. When the trauma involves the parent/caregiver as the perpetrator of the abuse, the support of a trusted parent/caregiver to help them regulate their strong emotions is lost; hence, children may experience overwhelming stress, with little ability to effectively communicate what they feel or need. These children may have very little sense of safety and security. These children are often left in a chronic state of anxiety and hyper vigilance. Many of their internal resources are consumed by the need to protect from further assault and survive from one day to the next. These defensives become so deeply ingrained in the personality. The defenses then comprise so much of who they are. They may never have the opportunity to address their own needs or feelings or to develop the basic life skills that are needed to function in this world.

COPING WITH TRAUMA

The most common effect of sexual abuse is Post Traumatic Stress Disorder. Symptoms can include withdrawn behavior, reenactment of the traumatic event, avoidance of circumstances that remind one of the events, and physiological hyper-reactivity. Variables that have a tremendous impact on the victim's emotional and behavioral outcomes have to do with the characteristics of the abuse (e.g., relationship to the perpetrator, the nature of the abusive acts, the use of force or threat, and frequency/duration of the abuse (Bennett, Hughes, & Luke, 2000; Williams, 1994; Trickett, Reiffman, Horowitz, & Putnam, 1997). Unfortunately, for many children, there may be exposed to continuous reminders of the abuse (e.g., continued contact with the perpetrator) and be unable to escape from the abusive situation. Though, the detrimental effects associated with child sexual abuse indicate that not all victims report disruptions in functioning, either in the short- or long-term.

CONCLUSION

It is important that research continue on the topic of the long-term effects of childhood sexual abuse. The severity of this issue and the significant implications it has on the lives of child and adult victims have been well established. With this knowledge, it is imperative that mental health professionals continue to expand their knowledge of best practices for survivors of child sexual abuse and be aware of all of the different types of treatment modalities. Mental health professionals have the obligation to adhere and attend to a client's preferences, cultural differences, and their own strengths and abilities while still providing scientifically grounded treatments for children who are enduring the of trauma of child sexual abuse.

REFERENCES

American Psychiatric Association (2015). *Diagnostic and Statistical Manual of Mental Disorders*, 4th Edition, Text Revision. Washington DC: APA.

Bennett, S. E., Hughes, H. M. and Luke, D. A. (2000). Heterogeneity in patterns of child sexual abuse, family functioning, and long-term adjustment. *Journal of Interpersonal Violence*, 75, 134-157.

Bol, C. (2008). Trauma focused therapy for the treatment of posttraumatic stress disorder in sexually abused children: A summary and evaluation of research. *Graduate Journal of Counseling Psychology*, 1(1), 147-158.

Bolen, R. M. (2001). *Child Sexual Abuse: Its Scope and Our Failure*. New York: Kluwer Academic/Plenum Publishers.

DiLillo, D. (2001). Interpersonal functioning among women reporting a history of childhood sexual abuse: Empirical findings and methodological issues. *Clinical Psychology Review*, 21, 553-576.

Fergusson, D. M., Horwood, L. J. and Lynskey, M. T. (1996). Childhood sexual abuse and psychiatric disorder in young adulthood: II. Psychiatric outcomes of childhood sexual abuse. *Journal of the American Academy of Child and Adolescent Psychiatry*, 35(10), 1365-1374.

Finkelhor, D. (1994). Current information on the scope and nature of child abuse. *The Future of Children*, 4, 31-53.

Finkelhor, D. and Browne, A., (1985). The traumatic impact of child sexual abuse: A conceptualization. *American Journal of Orthopsychiatry*, Vol. 55 (4), 530-541.

Garber, J. and Flynn, C. (2001). Predictors of depressive cognitions in young adolescents. *Cognitive Therapy and Research*, 4, 353-375.

Good, B. E. (2002). Childhood maltreatment and negative cognitive styles: A quantitative and qualitative review. *Clinical Psychology Review*, 22, 223-246.

Hankin, B. L., Abramson, L. Y. and Siler, M. (2001). A prospective test of the hopelessness theory of depression in adolescence. *Cognitive Therapy and Research*, 5, 607-632.

Kendall-Tackett, K. A., Williams, L. M. and Finkelhor, D. (1993). Impact of sexual abuse on children. *Psychological Bulletin*, 113, 164-180.

King, N., Tonge, B. and Mullen, P. (2000). Treating sexually abused children with posttraumatic stress symptoms: A randomized clinical trial. *Journal of the American Academy of Child and Adolescent Psychiatry*, 39, 1347-1355.

Knutson, J. F. (1995). Psychological characteristics of maltreated children: putative risk factors and consequences. *Annual Review of Psychology*, 46, 401-431.

Maltz, W. (2002). Treating the sexual intimacy concerns of sexual abuse survivors. *Sexual and Relationship Therapy*, 17(4), 321-327.

Miller, J. G. (1978). *Living systems*. New York: McGraw-Hill.

Putnam, F. (2003). Ten-year research update review. Child sexual abuse. *Journal of the American Academy of Child and Adolescent Psychiatry*, 42, 269-278.

Neumann, D. A., Houskamp, B. M., Pollock, V. E. and Briere, J. (1996). The long term sequelae of childhood sexual abuse in women: a meta-analytic review. *Child Maltreatment*, 1, 6-16.

Stein, M. B., Walker, J. R., Anderson, Geri, Hazen, A. L. (1996). *The American Journal of Psychiatry* 153.2 275-7.

Trickett, P. K., Reiffman, A., Horowitz, L. A. and Putman, F. W. (1997). Characteristics of sexual abuse trauma and the prediction of developmental outcomes. In: D. C. S. Toth (Ed.), *Rochester Symposium on Developmental Psychopathology: Developmental perspectives on trauma* (Vol. 8, pp. 289-314). Rochester, NY: University of Rochester.

Toth, S. L., Maughan, A., Manly, J. T., Spagnola, M. and Cicchetti, D. (2002). The relative efficacy of two interventions in altering maltreated preschool children's representational models: Implications for attachment theory. *Development and Psychopathology*, 14, 877-908.

US Department of Health and Human Services, National Center on Child Abuse and Neglect, National Child Abuse and Neglect Data System. (2012). *Child maltreatment 2012*. Washington, DC: US Government Printing Office.

US Department of Health and Human Services, Administration on Children and Families. *Child maltreatment 2012*. Retrieved from http://www.acf. hhs.gov/programs/cb/research-data technology/statistic/research/childmal treatment.

Vogeltanz, N. D., Wilsnack, S. C., Harris, T. R., Wilsnack, R. W., Wonderlich, S. A., Kristjanson, A. F. (1999). Prevalence and risk factors for childhood sexual abuse in women: National survey findings. *Child Abuse and Neglect*, 23:579-592.

Williams, L. M. (1994). Recall of childhood trauma: A prospective study of women's memories of child sexual abuse. *Journal of Consulting and Clinical Psychology*, Vol. 62(6), 1167-1176.

BIOGRAPHICAL SKETCH

Name: **Allison N. Sinanan, PhD, MSW**
Affiliation: Stockton University
Date of Birth: 12/08
Education: PhD in Social Work, MSW
Address: 101 Vera King Farris Drive, Galloway NJ

Research and Professional Experience: Dr. Allison N. Sinanan is an Associate Professor of Social Work at Stockton University in Galloway, New Jersey. She also currently serves as the coordinator for the BSW program. Dr. Sinanan's scholarly interests include examining child maltreatment recurrence and oppression and discrimination of minority populations. Dr. Sinanan teaches a range of undergraduate courses in the social work program, including: Introduction to Social, Race; Ethnicity and Diversity; and Theory and Methods Practice Courses. She also teaches a general studies course titled "Effects of Media on Children." Dr. Sinanan received her Ph.D. from Fordham University and an MSW from Adelphi University.

Publications Last 3 Years:

Tang, C. M. and Sinanan, A. and (accepted). Change in parenting behaviors from infancy to early childhood: Its impact on child behavior. A quantitative analysis. *Journal of Family Social Work.*

Sinanan, A. (2015). Trauma and Treatment of Child Sexual Abuse. *Journal of Trauma and Treatment.* S4:024. doi:10.4172/2167-1222.S4-024.

Sinanan, A. (2012). Still Here: African American Male Perceptions of Social and Academic Engagement at a Four-Year, Predominately White Institution of Higher Learning in Southern New Jersey. *Sage Open*, 2, 1-7.

Sinanan, A. (2012). Is TANF Creating Economic Dependency Among its Recipients? *International Journal of Humanities and Social Science,* 2 (24), 1-5.

Sinanan, A. (2011). The Impact of Child, Family, and Child Protective Services Factors on Reports of Child Abuse Recurrence. *Journal of Child Sexual Abuse*, 20, (6) 675-676.

Sinanan, A. (2011). Bridging the Gap of Teacher Education of Child Abuse. *The Journal of Educational Foundation*, 25, 3-4.

In: Sexual Abuse   ISBN: 978-1-63484-509-0
Editor: Olivia Parsons   © 2016 Nova Science Publishers, Inc.

Chapter 5

INVISIBLE VICTIMS: A REVIEW OF THE LITERATURE ON MALE SEXUAL ABUSE

Jennifer M. Foster[*]

Department of Counselor Education and Counseling Psychology,
Western Michigan University, MI, US

ABSTRACT

Child sexual abuse (CSA) is a pervasive global problem (Johnson, 2004). Although boys frequently experience sexual abuse, a disparate amount of attention has been given to male victims in the empirical literature. The vast majority of research on CSA includes predominately adult females and their recollections of CSA (Sorsoli, Kia-Keating & Grossman, 2008; Wilhite, 2015). Research samples with only females or with few men represented are extremely limited in their generalizability. Although there are numerous similarities between male and female victims, recent research has uncovered several distinct differences (Hopton & Huta, 2013). This review of the literature addresses the gap in current knowledge and understanding of male sexual abuse by exploring: (a) the prevalence of male sexual abuse, (b) victim and perpetrator characteristics, (c) disclosure, (d) short- and long-term outcomes for male survivors, (e) treatment, and (f) the healing journey.

[*] Correspondence concerning this article should be addressed to Jennifer M. Foster, Department of Counselor Education and Counseling Psychology, Western Michigan University, 3102 Sangren Hall, Kalamazoo, MI 49008 USA (email: Jennifer.Foster@wmich.edu).

INTRODUCTION

Child sexual abuse (CSA) is a pervasive societal problem around the world (Johnson, 2004). CSA is defined as "a type of maltreatment that refers to the involvement of the child in sexual activity to provide sexual gratification or financial benefit to the perpetrator, including contacts for sexual purposes, molestation, statutory rape, prostitution, pornography, exposure, incest, or other sexually exploitative activities" (USDHSS, 2013, p. 121). Sexual abuse includes contact and noncontact sexually abusive acts that are both overt and covert in nature. Overt abuse is "openly sexual" such as a fondling or penetration. Conversely, covert abuse is sexual in nature but more difficult to identify such as an offender undressing within view of a child or making sexual comments to a minor (Wilhite, 2015, p. 7). To date, there is no single agreed upon definition of sexual abuse, and each state has its own legal definition of CSA within civil and criminal statutes. This lack of a uniform definition is a challenge for clinicians and researchers (Foster & Carson, 2013).

Recent statistics indicate that there has been a 62% decrease in *reported* incidents of sexual abuse in the United States since the 1990s. Yet, it is clear the problem has not disappeared with 62,939 new cases of CSA reported in 2012 (USDHSS). This number does not include children who do not disclose as well as those whose abuse is not reported. Prevalence statistics try to capture this larger group, with the most commonly cited statistic estimating that 1 in 4 females and 1 in 6 males are sexually abused before the age of 18 (Centers for Disease Prevention and Control, 2005).

Although boys frequently experience sexual abuse, a disparate amount of attention has been given to male victims in the empirical literature. The vast majority of research on CSA includes predominately adult females and is focused on their recollections of childhood sexual abuse (Sorsoli, Kia-Keating & Grossman, 2008; Wilhite, 2015). Research samples with only females or with few men represented are extremely limited in their generalizability. Although there are numerous similarities between male and female victims, new research has uncovered several distinct differences (Hopton & Huta, 2013). The lack of research with male victims has created a problem of invisibility and misunderstanding. As a result, professional helpers are limited in their knowledge of key issues related to male victims as well as evidence-based treatments.

In addition to little attention in peer-reviewed literature, males are rarely acknowledged by society. Despite some efforts to raise awareness, the

American culture continues to struggle with acceptance of male victims of sexual abuse. This may be in part "because the experience stands in stark contrast to the notion of masculinity, damaging men's sense of power, control, and invulnerability" (Kia-Keating, Grossman, Sorsoli & Epstein, 2005, p. 169). These societal norms are especially problematic as they inhibit disclosure, promote concealment, and make the road to recovery arduous for male victims. Thus, there is a distinct need both among helping professionals and society to recognize and understand the experiences of males who have experienced sexual abuse.

In an effort to address the gap in current knowledge and understanding, this chapter provides a review of the literature on male sexual abuse, including: (a) the prevalence of male sexual abuse, (b) victim and perpetrator characteristics, (c) disclosure, (d) short- and long-term outcomes for male survivors, (e) treatment, and (f) the healing journey.

PREVALENCE OF MALE SEXUAL ABUSE

Prevalence rates of CSA vary widely both in the United States and abroad. Several variables affect prevalence rates, including the targeted population, the type of data analyzed, and the definition of sexual abuse. Some populations report rates of abuse (including sexual abuse) that are significantly higher than the general population, such individuals who are homeless, inpatient psychiatric patients, and sexual perpetrators (Connolly & Woollons, 2008). A recent study estimated that 1 in 10 people in the United States are sexually abused with 25% of victims being male (Perez-Fuentes, Olfson, Villegas, Morcillo, Wang & Blanco, 2013). Other research has focused on the prevalence of CSA on a global scale. For example, a meta-analysis of studies conducted in 20 countries reported that approximately 8% of men and 20% of women have been sexually abused. The researchers concluded that CSA was much more prevalent globally than formerly believed (Pereda, Guilera, Forns, & Gómez-Benito, 2009).

The aforementioned prevalence rates indicate that sexual abuse is higher among females. However, there are a number of factors that may skew the rates. First, males are expected to be strong and capable of self-protection. Males who feel weak, vulnerable, and ashamed following abuse may not disclose. Second, males may be embarrassed about being abused by another male or fear that they will be labeled a homosexual, which could also impede disclosure (Pereda et al., 2009). Third, traditional definitions of sexual abuse may not reflect males' experiences and beliefs about what occurred, especially if the perpetrator was a female. As a result, some males may not consider their experience abusive and may even view it as a positive experience in becoming a man. As a result, these factors have the strong potential to impact rates of disclosure as well as self-identification as a victim of abuse.

CHARACTERISTICS OF MALE VICTIMS AND THEIR PERPETRATORS

In addition to prevalence rates, researchers have identified characteristics of male sexual abuse victims and their offenders. However, these characteristics are restricted to reported cases of sexual abuse. As mentioned earlier, many males never disclose the abuse, thus there may be a difference between the characteristics of male victims who disclose abuse and those who do not (Holmes & Slap, 1998; Valente, 2005). Along with this, a major limitation is recent research on the characteristics of male sexual abuse victims has not been conducted. Many current articles continue to cite studies that were conducted in the 1990s. Despite these limitations, this section will explore the mean age of abuse, environmental risks, and family characteristics of victims as well as qualities of offenders of male sexual abuse.

Male Victims

Research widely varies with regards to mean age of first sexual abuse experience for males. Many studies are limited in generalizability by their small, homogeneous samples. According to Holmes and Slap (1998), the existing large scale studies conducted in the 1990s indicated a mean age of 9.8 and a median age of 10 for boys' initial sexual abuse experiences. Spiegel's (2003) review of numerous studies estimates the mean age to be between 8 and 10 with 28% below the age of 7, including some who were abused while they were still preverbal.

Along with age at the onset of abuse, researchers have examined environmental commonalities among males who have been sexually abused. Research indicates that there is a high correlation between adverse childhood experiences, such as growing up in a markedly dysfunctional household and child sexual abuse or neglect (Dong et al., 2004). Specifically, researchers found that boys who lived with only one parent, typically a mother, or no parents, were at a higher risk of experiencing sexual abuse (Holmes & Slap, 1998; Moody, 1999).

There are also multiple parental factors that increase the risk of sexual abuse. Boys who had parents that were divorced, remarried, or separated and boys who had parents that had a history of alcohol abuse and criminal behavior were at an increased risk of experiencing CSA (Holmes & Slap, 1998). In many cases, these families also had parents that were physically abusive, were of a lower socioeconomic status, and/or unemployed or worked in unskilled labor positions (Holmes & Slap; Moody, 1999). Furthermore, previous research indicated that about half of sexually abused boys had mothers that received public assistance (Holmes & Slap). If the sexual abuse perpetrator was a family relative, the boy victim was two times more likely to come from a low socioeconomic household (Holmes & Slap).

One of the greatest risk factors for sexual abuse in males is the presence of abuse of a sibling (Moody, 1999). Research has shown that boys who had a family member who was sexually abused were 15 times more likely to be sexually abused themselves (Holmes & Slap, 1998). Although most girls are sexually abused by known male perpetrators, male victims of sexual abuse are more likely to be abused by an unknown perpetrator at a location other than the child's home (Murray, 2000).

Offenders

As a society, we often hold incorrect images of those who sexually abuse children. Perpetrators of sexual abuse are a diverse group, representing various ages, genders, ethnicities, socioeconomic levels, sexual orientations, relationship statuses, and experiences with children (i.e., those with or without their own children) (Finkelhor, 2008; Murray, 2000). Studies have identified four common characteristics (in which one or more tend to be present) among those who perpetrate CSA, including: poor emotional regulation, social skills deficits, abnormal sexual arousal patterns, and cognitive distortions (which includes faulty beliefs about their offending) (Ward & Beech, 2005), and most acts of CSA can be conceptualized as offenders acting out of a need for power and control. Some perpetrators use children as substitutes for adults within the family system, others abuse both within and outside of the family, and still others use children to meet their sexual needs because they find children less threatening than adults. Further, there are offenders who are sadistic and violent; whereas others are situational opportunists. Lastly, most sexual perpetrators abuse more than one child, and following incarceration there is a high recidivism rate (and even higher estimated reoffense rate), although this varies by the nature of the sexual offense (Przybylski, 2014). Conversely, juvenile offenders have a lower recidivism rate (9-13% after 59 months) (Lobanov-Rostovsky, 2014), which can be further lowered through treatment interventions.

Research has strongly indicated that the majority of sexual abuse perpetrators are male, and men make up 96% of reported incidents of CSA (Finkelhor, 2008; Finkelhor et al., 2008). A common assumption is that all men who offend were sexually abused as children. Although some perpetrators experienced sexual abuse (see Glasser et al., 2001), research indicates that there are different pathways to juvenile as well as adult offending (Przybylski, 2014).

Males are not the only perpetrators of sexual abuse. Recent studies indicate that female perpetrators are more common than was previously believed (Finkelhor et al., 2008; Snyder, 2000) with women committing 4-5% of offenses (Cortoni & Hansen, 2005; Sandler & Freeman, 2009). Female perpetrators of sexual abuse tend to target children below the age of six that they know and have easy access to (Crossen-Tower, 2009; Finkelhor et al., 2008). As a result, sexual abuse by women in a caretaking role is likely to go unnoticed. Moreover, abuse by non-caregiving females may be underreported due to the cultural assumption that males should be able to protect themselves from harm.

Another common misconception is that only adults are sexual offenders. Child on child sexual abuse is extremely prevalent with one study indicating that juveniles commit approximately 23% of sexual abusive acts (Finkelhor et al., 2008). Sibling sexual abuse may be the most common type of sexual abuse that occurs within families (Welfare, 2008). Further, sibling sexual abuse (e.g., biological siblings, step-siblings, adoptive/foster siblings) often includes violence, force, and penetration (Tremblay, Hebert, & Piche, 1999). Victims of sibling sexual abuse are even less apt to disclose than children whose abuse is by other family members (Carlson, Maciol, & Schneider, 2006). For a comprehensive review of research on juvenile and adult sex offenders see the National Criminal Justice Association's 2104 report titled Sex Offender Management, Assessment, and Planning Initiative.

For males who have been sexually abused, the gender (and perhaps the age) of the perpetrator often makes a difference with how the sexual abuse is perceived. Sexual abuse between a boy and an adult female may be viewed as not having a negative effect or even in a positive light; whereas sexual abuse between a boy and adult male is viewed with abhorrence (Duncan & Williams, 1998). Further, sexual abuse of a young male by another male is considered to be a violation of the traditional gender norms and a threat to the victim's masculine identity. Thus the gender of the offender may impact a boy's willingness to disclose, which is explored in the following section.

THE RISK OF DISCLOSURE FOR MALE VICTIMS

Disclosure refers to the act of sharing the secret of one's abuse. It is important to understand children's perspective as they weigh the risks and benefits of disclosure. Narratives written by children revealed the arduous disclosure process, which included feelings of fear, embarrassment, isolation, shame, and responsibility (Foster, 2011; Foster & Hagedorn, 2014a, 2014b). "When a child tells that he or she has been sexually abused, the private is changed to public and professional attention is drawn to more intense personal conflict and turmoil." (Durham, 2003, p. 316). The following section details both the specific obstacles faced by males that hinder or prevent disclosure and the familial and societal reactions to discovery of male CSA.

Obstacles that Jeopardize Disclosure

For male victims of CSA, the act of disclosure is fraught with obstacles, some of which are different than those experienced by females. Many boys report feeling ashamed that they were not able to stop the abuse, and numerous adult men who did not disclose as children remained silent in order to protect themselves from the familial and societal stigma. Research has uncovered several predominate factors that hinder disclosure, including: societal factors, feeling of responsibility, perpetrator factors, and fear of being viewed as a homosexual or perpetrator. Each of these is explored below.

First, disclosure for male victims in the United States is impacted by the patriarchal nature of western society, which has intrinsically shaped gender role expectations (Alaggia & Millington, 2008). Society demands that males be fearless, powerful, strong, in control, and dominant. Sexual abuse, by its very nature, is the antithesis of these strongly held societal beliefs. Thus the norms of western culture that refuse to acknowledge men can be "victims" increase distress for males who have experienced sexual abuse (Wilhite, 2015).

Besides societal factors, the natural egocentrism in young males leads many to assume responsibility for their assault (Goodman-Brown, Edelstein, Goodman, Jones, & Gordon, 2003). Boys' sense of responsibility may be exasperated by their compliance with the abuse. Furthermore, many boys experience an erection or orgasm during abuse, which the literature has termed as body betrayal. This experience can be very distressing and result in feelings of guilt, responsibility, and confusion (Alaggia & Millington, 2008).

Along with a sense of responsibility, the male victims' relationship with perpetrators can make disclosure exceedingly difficult if not impossible. Some perpetrators make direct and indirect threats in an attempt to silence their victims (Murray, 2000; Oz, 2005). Such threats may include bodily harm or fatal consequences to the victim and/or his family members. Other perpetrators tell children if they disclose, they will be blamed or punished, which many victims believe to be true.

Other children have more complicated relationship with their perpetrators, such as being in a position of dependence (e.g., perpetrator is their father or caregiver). If the perpetrator is a relative of the victim then the rate of disclosure decreases (Ulman, 2005), and males are least likely to disclose if the perpetrator is a parent (Goodman-Brown et al., 2003). Disclosure is also complicated when boys feel love or acceptance from the offender. One study interviewing survivors found they did not disclose the abuse due to a sense of feeling special, which was related to the grooming behaviors used by the offenders including attention, gifts, and money (Alaggia & Millington, 2008). When positive or protective feelings develop or the child is reliant on the perpetrator for basic needs, disclosure is an excruciating decision for a child (Foster, 2011; Foster & Hagedorn, 2014a).

In addition to perpetrator factors, some males do not disclose abuse or they delay disclosure out of fear of how others will perceive them. For example, some men may worry that because they were sexually abused as a child, others will think that they will now abuse children. Although many sex offenders have histories of child maltreatment, the majority of boys who are sexually abused do not grow up to be perpetrators.

Another fear boys' have is that people will perceive them as homosexual if their offender was also a male. Furthermore, if they experienced pleasure they may question their sexual identity. Conversely, men who are sexually abused by females face a number of unique challenges related to disclosure and the perceptions of others. Males may worry that they will be perceived as weak for not stopping the abuse or fear that they will be accused of initiating the sexual relationship (Holmes & Slap, 1998; Romano & DeLuca, 2001). Thus males may not disclose out of fear of judgment and negative reactions of others (Priebe, 2008). Recently more attention has been brought to these types of cases, and popular culture has depicted female-on-male sexual assault as "every man's dream." Disclosure is very unlikely when boys view abuse by an adult female as a positive experience that helped develop their masculinity (Hopton & Huta, 2013).

Each of the above fears and obstacles makes disclosure for males especially complicated and risky. Many boys and adult men only disclose when they are directly asked during a therapeutic encounter (Valente, 2005). Yet, young males are rarely asked if they have been a victim of sexual abuse by helpers and other mandated reporters, which exasperates the problem of male sexual abuse being undisclosed (Lab, Feigenbaum, & DeSilva, 2000).

In sum, "the tendency for males to never disclose their abuse and face difficulties from others accepting the significance of these events means men and boys remain neglected and silenced victims of sexual abuse" (Wilhite, 2015, p. 1). More research is needed to investigate the risks and benefits males experience during the disclosure process in order to create a climate within families, schools, and communities that encourages and supports boys who reveal sexual abuse. The following section explores the responses males receive to their abuse disclosure.

Reactions to Male Disclosure

There is scant literature on the reactions of parents and the community in regards to the disclosure of male sexual abuse. At the familial level, preliminary findings have indicated that when parents learned about the abuse, they emphasized hyper masculinity in their sons, in part due to their fear that the experience of abuse by an adult male would lead to homosexuality (McGuffey, 2008). In an attempt to reconstruct their sons' sexual identities, parents relied on emotional detachment, athleticism, and promotion of heterosexuality to aid in reaffirmation. This may be emphasized even more in Latino and African American cultures, which stress adherence to traditional gender norms (Levant et al., 2003), and the need to conform is felt strongly by boys of color who are sexually abused (Kia-Keating et al., 2005).

Along with the familial reactions to abuse disclosure, research has started to uncover community reactions. Durham (2003) interviewed males ages 15 to

24 who were victims of CSA on their experiences with the legal system following the disclosure of the abuse. The researcher found that the boys endured rigorous cross-examinations by the defense council and were accused of lying about their abuse (Durham, 2003). Other research has attested that boys who disclose sexual abuse experience rejection and teasing from their peers (West, 1998). A more recent study of men's narratives indicated when they disclosed they were more likely to be encouraged by their family as well as peers to act violently in order to prove toughness (Kia-Keating et al., 2005). The supportive and believing reaction to a male's disclosure has the potential to have a healing impact; whereas, a negative reaction often leads to further wounding and silencing. For boy victims and adult male survivors there are numerous potential outcomes following their abuse. The next section of this chapter discusses these ramifications.

OUTCOMES FOR MALE SURVIVORS

Child sexual abuse has the potential for a multitude of short- and long-term consequences for both male and female victims (Hebert, Tremblay, Parent, Daignault & Piche, 2006; Johnson, 2004). This section begins with an overview of the empirical literature on children in general, and then focuses on the research specific to males.

Children greatly differ in their responses in the immediate aftermath of the CSA, with approximately one-third of children presenting as asymptomatic; whereas, approximately half are diagnosed with severe psychological distress (Adler-Nevo & Manassis, 2005; Anderson & Hiersteiner, 2008). Many children experience difficulty in one or more of the following domains: social, cognitive/academic, physical, spiritual, and emotional (Goldfinch, 2009; Tomlinson, 2008). Specific problems experienced by child victims of sexual abuse include: internalizing and externalizing behaviors, anxiety, depression, delinquent behavior, attention problems, cognitive deficiencies, mood disorders, posttraumatic stress disorder, and eating disorders (Brack, Heufner & Handwerk, 2012; Doerfler, Toscano & Connor, 2009; Horner, 2010).

There are several factors that impact children's response to abuse and recovery, which include age/developmental stage at the time of the abuse, abuse duration and severity, level of family support, relationship to perpetrator, and reactions of others to their disclosure (Webster, 2001; Welfare, 2008). When interventions are provided soon after disclosure, most children experience a reduction in symptoms. Furthermore, early intervention has been linked to fewer long-term negative outcomes (Cohen, Mannarino, & Knudsen, 2005; Lataster et al., 2006; Parker, Fourt, Langmuir, Dalton, & Classen, 2007).

Recently researchers have focused their attention on the impact of CSA on boys. First, research indicates a correlation between ADHD, depression, and sexual abuse in males (Sonnby, Aslund, Leppert & Nilsson, 2011). Additionally, boys with a history of sexual abuse are more likely to engage in unprotected sexual intercourse, cause a pregnancy, and have multiple sexual partners than boys who were not sexually abused (Homma, Wang, Saewyc & Kishor, 2012). Moreover, there is a relationship between experiences of childhood sexual and physical abuse and later criminal behavior. Although this finding was attributed to both males and females, the effect of sexual abuse on adolescent offending was more pronounced for males (Watts & McNulty, 2013).

The literature has generally attributed more externalizing behaviors (e.g., fighting, stealing, and destruction of property) to male victims (Horner, 2010), but not all studies support this. For example, Coohey (2010) noted that during early adolescence (ages 11-14) boys were more likely than sexually abused girls to have clinically significant internalizing behaviors. He hypothesized that these may evolve into more externalizing behaviors later in adolescence. The aforementioned studies point to the potential for numerous negative outcomes for males in their preadolescent and teen years. Negative consequences often continue into adulthood when trauma is unresolved. These long-term ramifications are discussed in the next section.

Long-Term Consequences of Sexual Abuse

For some survivors, the road to healing is long and arduous. Challenges can arise at multiple points across the lifespan, impacting one's overall health and wellbeing. For example, adult survivors of CSA have a higher risk of suicide attempts, substance abuse, depression, and marital problems, including higher divorce rates (Colman & Widom, 2004; Dube et al., 2005). These risks were elevated when either penetration was involved or when the offender was a female.

Several studies have focused specifically on outcomes for male victims of sexual abuse. One study identified five variables that increased male suicide attempts, including: force during the sexual abuse, duration of the sexual abuse, level of depressive symptoms, high conformity to masculine norms, and suicidal ideation (Easton, Renner & O'Leary, 2013). Another study surveyed 280 heterosexual adult men with a history of CSA and found a correlation between the severity of the abuse and an earlier age of drinking initiation, elevated levels of current alcohol consumption, and number of sexual partners (Schraufnagel, Davis, George & Norris, 2010). A third study (N = 25) examined the men's perspectives of sexual abuse resulting in eight life areas that were affected: social, psychological, physical, sexual, familial, sense of self, relation to men, and relation to women (Ray, 2001). Many of the men in this study reported feelings of guilt for being a male. A fourth study reported that male survivors indicated higher levels of interpersonal sensitivity, anxiety, depression and phobic anxiety than sexually abused women (Gold, Lucenko, Elhai, Swingle & Sellers, 1999). A fifth study reported re-victimized men had significantly higher levels of PTSD, depression, feelings of hostility, and general distress (Aoesved, Long, & Voller, 2011).

The above research represents just a few of the studies that suggest the possibility of negative ramifications for sexually abused males both immediately following the abuse and in later developmental stages. Yet, counseling can lead to improved outcomes, including symptom reduction, improved relationships, and posttraumatic growth.

TREATMENT FOR SEXUALLY ABUSED MALES

Counseling for Boys using Trauma Focused Cognitive Behavioral Therapy

Although there are numerous treatment options for child victims of sexual abuse, Trauma Focused Cognitive Behavioral Therapy (TF-CBT) has been deemed statistically superior to other treatment methods (e.g., nondirective approaches and play therapy) and placebo for children who have experienced various types of trauma based on symptom reduction at the end of treatment and in one year follow-ups (e.g., Cohen et al., 2005; Silverman et al., 2008). TF-CBT addresses trauma related symptoms, including dysfunctional cognitions about the trauma and trauma related fears (Cohen & Mannarino, 2000). The model utilizes gradual trauma exposure and provides an avenue for children to record their thoughts, feelings, and beliefs about their experiences in a written narrative.

TF-CBT can be implemented in both individual and group treatment settings, and it frequently includes a family component in which the child shares his or her trauma narrative with a non-offending parent or caregiver (Cohen & Mannarino, 2008; NCTSN, 2004). Research indicates that group counseling may have additional advantages for clients with a sexual abuse history, including decreasing loneliness and improving connection with others in a safe environment (Lundqvist, Hansson, & Svedin, 2009; Nisbet-Wallis, 2002). This may be especially important for boys who identify feeling alone and different from other boys (Garnefski& Arends, 1998).

TF-CBT begins with developing a therapeutic relationship. Many children fear their counselor will break their trust or victimize them again (McGregor et al., 2006). If children's fears are ignored, rapport cannot be established (Foster & Hagedorn, 2014b). Creating a healthy relationship built upon trust takes time and is essential for positive therapeutic outcomes (Gil, 2006; Kaminer, 2006). When working with boys, counselors need to establish and maintain healthy boundaries and address openly any sexual behaviors that occur in sessions (Hall, 2007). Once a safe, trusting relationship has been established, children can begin to organize and integrate their traumatic memories through writing a trauma narrative (Foa, Molnar, & Cashman, 1995).

While processing their narrative, children are challenged to explore their cognitions (Foa & Rothebaum, 1998; Kaminer, 2006). Counselors help boys explore thoughts related to masculinity, sexual orientation, and their responses to the abuse (e.g., physical, emotional, cognitive). Cognitive-behavioral techniques are used to explore boys' concerns and challenge unhelpful beliefs (e.g., guilt, shame, and personal responsibility) (Cohen & Mannarino, 2008, NCTSN, 2004).

Within the trauma narrative, it is not uncommon for children to discuss past, current, and future fears related to their abuse experiences (Foster, 2011; Foster & Hagedorn, 2014b). Boys may recall feeling afraid during the abuse. Additionally, boys may have feared that they would not be believed or that they would be blamed or punished. They may also report ongoing fears regarding re-victimization by the same or a new perpetrator. Additionally, boys may fear that they will be labeled by others as weak for not stopping the abuse or as a homosexual if the perpetrator was male. Moreover, boys may worry that being abused by a male makes them a homosexual, especially if they experienced pleasure (Moody, 1999). Furthermore, boys may express confusion about an erection or orgasm during an experience that they may have also felt afraid or manipulated (Valente, 2005). Counselors can address these and other fears with boys and help them regain a sense of personal safety and trust in others (Foster; Foster & Hagedorn, 2014b).

In addition to addressing fears, counselors can help boys explore direct and indirect messages from family and culture that may communicate they need to be tough and get over their abuse. These messages can be harmful and may inhibit boys from fully expressing their feelings of sadness and loss (Sandoval et al., 2009). Counselors need to be aware of their own biases about male sexual abuse. For example, some research has indicated that counselors are more likely to question the validity of sexual abuse by female perpetrators, which boys are more likely than girls to experience (Gore-Felton et al., 2000).

Finally, TF-CBT values and promotes the inclusion of non-offending parents and caregivers in therapy. Inclusion of parents leads to improved treatment outcomes (Cohen, Mannarino, & Deblinger, 2006; Cohen & Mannarino, 2000; Feather & Ronan, 2009; Lanktree & Briere, 2008; Silverman et al., 2008) and strengthens family relationships (Sheinberg & True, 2008). When working with boys, counselors need to find ways to support their parents or caregivers who are often experiencing their own distress. The following section provides specific ideas about how to support boys' parents.

Supporting Boys' Nonoffending Parents and Caregivers

Counselors need to be aware that boys' parents may not be in tune with their sons emotional needs (Nilsson, Gustafsson, & Svedin, 2012) or may consciously or unconsciously maintain a code of silence about the abuse (Kia-Keating et al., 2005). Counselors need to educate parents and caregivers about boys' need to emote and give specific suggestions to help boys to express their feelings at home.

Counselors may also need to assist and support parents if their son's abuse becomes public, helping them navigate challenges such as stigma for being a victim or labeled a homosexual (Coohey, 2010). Parents of boys who have been sexually abused by a male often wonder if the sexual abuse will lead to homosexuality (McGuffey, 2008). Although there is not substantial research to support this assertion, it is important for parents to communicate acceptance of their children. Counselors can share with parents that "sexuality is a fluid process and that all forms of sexual expression are valid as long as they are between consenting adults" (McGuffey, p. 223). Requiring parents to participate in individual or group counseling allows for parents to receive psycho-education about sexual abuse, specifically the ways boys may be affected. Additionally, parents can explore their reactions to their sons' sexual abuse and learn ways of better supporting them. If TF-CBT is utilized, parents can be prepared for the family session in which the boy shares his narrative about his abuse experiences. For more information on working with the family using TF-CBT and the trauma narrative intervention see Foster (2014).

In sum, treatment for boys with a history of sexual abuse must address presenting symptoms and reduce the likelihood of future negative outcomes. Therapy with this population is not without unique challenges. During the beginning treatment, it is not uncommon for boys' to experience elevated symptomology (e.g., anxiety) and slowed progress, which may lead to ending treatment prematurely. Dropout rates are especially high for sexually abused children (Chasson et al., 2008). Parents may end treatment if their child expresses reluctance to address the sexual abuse and/or experiences an increase in symptoms. Counselors can work to reduce the likelihood of premature dropout by preparing children and their parents for the challenges of treatment. Despite the hurdles associated with counseling boys, healing can and does occur (Perry, 2009).

Counseling Men

While early interventions are often successful in reducing children's presenting symptoms, the devastating effects of sexual abuse can be long reaching when trauma is unresolved. Survivors with unprocessed trauma may experience numerous intrapersonal and/or interpersonal challenges in adulthood (Cohen et al., 2005; Lataster et al., 2006; Parker et al., 2007). A large number of adults (on average 50% of women and 28% of men) who present for therapy have a history of sexual abuse (Read, Goodman, Morrison, Ross, & Aderhold, 2004). Yet adults rarely identify CSA as their presenting problem. Rencken (2000) found that adults who were sexually abused as children sought counseling for the following reasons: depression, anxiety, fears, eating disorders, body image problems, dissociative patterns, somatic concerns, and interpersonal problems such as difficulty with intimacy. Clients may not understand or acknowledge the potential connection between their current challenges and sexual abuse history.

Men face experience additional challenges when seeking counseling. One of the largest challenges is locating counseling services that specialize in the treatment of men with a sexual abuse history (Hopton & Huta, 2013). This is an important concern as poorly conducted treatment can be especially damaging to adult abuse victims and may lead to increased suffering (Schauer et al., 2004). On the other hand, effective counseling is extremely powerful (Little & Hamby, 1999). The following sections review models of treatment designed specifically for men, how to address men's unique concerns in counseling, and group work with sexually abused men.

Models of Treatment for Male Sexual Abuse

Two treatment models have been developed specifically for male survivors of sexual abuse: The Four Phase Model (Crowder, 1995) and the SAM Model (Spiegel, 2003). In the Four Phase Model, there are four main components to treatment: the breaking silence phase, the victim phase, the survivor phase, and the thriver phase. Coping and decision making are emphasized. There is an opportunity to explore the past (grieving losses) but also look ahead to the future (developing a new identity).

The SAM Model (Spiegel, 2003) is both a practical and theoretical model. It was the first to create a theory of abuse dynamics and effects based solely on male victims and their personal experiences. The SAM Model includes a discussion of the response cycle that male victims experience following the abuse (Spiegel, 2003, p. 243). In his comprehensive text, Spiegel reviews the literature on male sexual abuse, the assumptions of the model, philosophy of practice, objectives for treatment, and specific interventions. Male survivors are supported as they explore their past, which begins with acknowledgement of abuse, and includes grieving losses and narrating one's story. Research on the SAM Model is needed to establish it as an evidence-based approach.

Tailoring Counseling to Address Men's Needs

With any theoretical approach, men need to know from the moment they enter a counseling office that CSA is something that they can talk about. This begins with asking directly about CSA on a written intake and following up with questions during an initial interview. Some men will not report CSA on an intake, particularly if they have never disclosed or do not perceive their experience as sexually abusive. Disclosure may be enhanced when men are provided with a list specific examples of sexually abusive acts with space for the client to respond to each with yes or no. It is vital for counselors to verbally follow up with men about this section of the intake, as many men leave this section blank or deny history of CSA.

When a history of sexual abuse is disclosed, counselors must listen with empathy. Counselors can then help clients consider in what ways and to what extent their history of CSA is currently impacting them. "Men who come to therapy with an acknowledged history of sexual abuse often represent the more clinically distressed end of the spectrum. When such men have no prior history of treatment, the clinical challenges are even greater" (Hall, 2007, p. 367-368).

Common presenting symptoms in adult males with a CSA history include: anxiety, depression (Gold et al., 1999), posttraumatic stress, suicidal ideations (Hopton & Huta, 2013), and substance abuse (Hopton & Huta; Schraufnage et al., 2010), which for some men was used as a coping mechanism to block abuse memories (Durham, 2003). Symptom assessment and strategies for reduction is an important part of counseling adult males. Men can explore their current coping strategies and learn new ways to managing feelings of stress and trauma memories. Counselors can also explore Ray's (2001) eight areas of life that are frequently affected by sexual abuse for men (discussed above), with emphasis on the most common challenges of trust, self-worth, and its impact on relationships.

Special attention must also be paid to the potential impact of CSA on sexual functioning (Bramblett & Darling, 1997; Hall, 2007; Long, Burnett, & Thomas, 2006). Research indicates that men with a CSA history are significantly more likely to experience sexual problems than their nonsexually abused peers (Holmes & Slap, 1998; Loeb et al., 2002). For example, sexually abused males are more likely to be involved in high risk sexual behavior, express gender role confusion, and experience difficulties with intimacy. Other potential sexual problems of male survivors include sexual avoidance, sexual addictions, compulsive masturbation, difficulty with arousal, rapid or delayed ejaculation, and erectile dysfunction (Long et al., 2006). Adolescent and young adult males interviewed about their sexual abuse expressed concerns about their sexuality following abuse by a male and also shared their concern that they could become a perpetrator (Durham, 2003). Specific treatment for sexual abuse survivors is only just emerging, and most interventions are created for adult females. Therefore, additional research is needed to uncover effective treatment for sexual concerns of men with a history of CSA (Hall, 2007).

Along with exploring sexual concerns, men can also be encouraged to explore internalized messages about masculinity as well as cultural messages about their abuse experiences in counseling (Grossman, Sorsoli, Kia-Keating, 2006). American culture frequently expects men to withhold emotions (except anger) and present themselves as strong protectors and providers. Counselors can help men new discover ways to express themselves and develop a new identity.

Group Interventions for Men

Groups for adult males with a CSA history may be especially helpful to validate the abuse experience and receive support. In the safety of the group men can express their thoughts and feelings related to how the sexual abuse impacted their view of self and others. Groups also provide an opportunity for men to explore ways that their past may be continuing to negatively influence their present functioning (e.g., negative coping, relationship problems). Men can be challenged to explore new ways of managing their emotions and connecting to others. Men may also benefit from experiential exercises that allow them to safely confront the perpetrator of the abuse, through empty chair or letter writing (Draucker & Martsolf, 2006). When conducted in a group format, group members could offer support during cathartic therapeutic exercises.

For men, sharing openly with others and receiving assistance may be especially difficult (Kia-Keating et al., 2005). The counseling process can help them "reconstruct what it means to be masculine" and identify ways to engage in healthy relationships (Kia-Keating et al., p. 183). Counseling for males who have been sexually abused needs to be tailored to meet their unique needs and match their experiences. Counseling provides a place for males to explore confusing, hurtful, and/or frightening abuse experiences in the safety of the therapeutic relationship. For many male survivors it is the beginning of their healing journey, which is explored in the next section.

THE HEALING JOURNEY: PREPARING FOR A POSITIVE FUTURE

Boys and men can take an active role in creating a positive future for themselves. The road to healing includes several important steps, including: disclosing the abuse, learning healthy coping skills, developing a sense of resiliency, and working through emotions (Kia-Keating et al., 2005). While these processes may be undertaken outside of the counseling relationship, they also coincide with the therapeutic process.

Disclosure is the first step. Earlier, the arduous decision to disclose was discussed as well as the potential for negative, unsupportive, or judgmental reactions. Despite these risks and obstacles, disclosure allows the survivor to share their secret and opens a door for the healing journey to begin. Once they are accompanied by a supportive, believing person, they are no longer alone.

Following disclosure, many survivors need to learn new ways of coping with the pain of the past. Establishing positive coping strategies is an essential step before exploring the details of the abuse in counseling. When males are ready to begin exploring their abuse, many discover their strengths and resiliency. These traits can be affirmed and developed further in counseling and other supportive relationships.

In addition to learning coping strategies and exploring the trauma, this is important to evaluate ones beliefs about masculinity. This process may involve deconstructing former ideas of conventional masculinity that do not fit with their view of self. Counselors have noted that many survivors in treatment "struggled with the expectations of conventional masculinity, particularly in the domains of expected toughness, stoicism, and sexual prowess" (Kia-Keating et al., 2005, p. 175). One of the ways that masculinity can be deconstructed is working through emotions related to the abuse, disclosure, and healing process. During this time of exploration, men have the opportunity to increase their ability to identify and share their feelings. A positive future can be a reality for every survivor, and counselors and supportive friends and family play an important role through instilling hope and accompanying men on their journey.

CONCLUSION

This chapter on male sexual abuse highlights several important findings related to the prevalence of male sexual abuse, victim and perpetrator characteristics, disclosure, short- and long-term outcomes for male survivors, treatment, and healing journey. Data on the prevalence of CSA asserts that numerous boys are sexually abused annually. Disclosure rates for males are extremely low, and disclosure is complicated by a number of factors. Although some males present with little to no symptoms following abuse, many are adversely affected. Male victims have to contend with familial and cultural reactions to male CSA, including disbelief, secrecy, shame, and stigma. Males may additionally struggle to find adequate support from family and friends.

Further, male victims are more likely than females to have difficulty locating counseling services that specialize in male sexual abuse.

In order to improve outcomes for sexually abused boys and adult male survivors, changes are needed. Evidence-based treatment approaches are lacking for adult males, and more research is needed to examine the effectiveness of models created for men such as the Spiegel's (2003) SAM model (Wilhite, 2015). Although specific evidence-based interventions have not been established, counseling in a group modality is a promising form of treatment that is time and cost effective and helps reduce shame and stigma, while providing social support. In addition to the need for evidence-based practices, there is an urgent need for counselors to receive training in the treatment of sexual abuse, which must include preparation for the unique needs of males.

Outcomes will be further improved for males when counselors engage with their communities to educate others about male sexual abuse. These advocacy efforts will help reduce stigma and provide accurate education. Simultaneously, counselors can help their communities develop child sexual abuse preventative efforts. Such efforts could teach community members how to identify warning signs of potential perpetrators as well as risk factors that may indicate a child has been sexually abused. Finally, more research is needed to understand how males perceive their sexual abuse experiences and journey towards wholeness and healing.

REFERENCES

Adler-Nevo, G., & Manassis, K. (2005). Psychosocial treatment of pediatric posttraumatic stress disorder: The neglected field of single-incident trauma. *Depression & Anxiety, 22*(4), 177-189.

Alaggia, R., & Millington, G. (2008). Male child sexual abuse: A phenomenology of betrayal. *Clinical Journal of Social Work, 36*(3), 265–275.

Anderson, K. M., & Hiersteiner, C. (2008). Recovering from childhood sexual abuse: Is a "storybook ending" possible? *American Journal of Family Therapy, 36*(5), 413-424. doi:10.1080/01926180701804592.

Aoesved, A., Long, P., & Voller, E. (2011). Sexual revictimization and adjustment in college men. *Psychology of Men and Masculinity, 12,* 285-296.

Brack, A., Heufner, J., & Handwerk, M. (2012). The impact of abuse and gender on psychopathology, behavioral disturbance, and psychotropic medication count for youth in residential treatment. *American Journal of Orthopsychiatry, 82,* 562-572.

Bramblett, J., & Darling, C. (1997). Sexual contacts: Experiences, thoughts, and fantasies of adult male survivors of child sexual abuse. *Journal of Sex and Marital Therapy, 23,* 305-316.

Centers for Disease Control and Prevention. (2005). *Adverse childhood experiences study: Data and statistics.* Atlanta, GA: Centers for Disease Control and Prevention, National Center for Injury Prevention and Control. Retrieved from http://www.cdc.gov/nccdphp/ace/prevalence. htm#table.

Carlson, B. E., Maciol, K., & Schneider, J. (2006). Sibling incest: Reports from forty-one survivors. *Journal of Child Sexual Abuse, 15*(4), 19-34.

Chasson, G. S., Vincent, J. P., & Harris, G. E. (2008). The use of symptom severity measured just before termination to predict child treatment dropout. *Journal of Clinical Psychology, 64*(7), 891-904. doi:10.1002/ jclp.20494.

Child Sexual Abuse Task Force and Research & Practice Core, National Child Traumatic Stress Network (NCTSN). (2004). *How to Implement Trauma-Focused Cognitive Behavioral Therapy.* Durham, NC: National Center for Child Traumatic Stress. Retrieved from http://www.nctsn.org/nccts/ nav.do?pid=ctr_top_trmnt.

Cohen, J. A., & Mannarino, A. P. (2000). Predictors of treatment outcome in sexually abused children. *Child Abuse and Neglect, 24,* 983–994. doi:10.1016/S0145-2134(00)00153-8.

Cohen, J. A., & Mannarino, A. P. (2008). Trauma-focused cognitive behavioral therapy for children and parents. *Child and Adolescent Mental Health, 13*(4), 158-162.

Cohen, J. A., Mannarino, A. P., & Deblinger, E. (2006). *Treating trauma and traumatic grief in children and adolescents.* NY: The Guilford Press.

Cohen, J. A., Mannarino, A. P., & Knudsen, K. (2005). Treating sexually abused children: 1 year follow-up of a randomized controlled trial. *Child Abuse and Neglect, 29*(2), 135-145. doi:10.1016/j.chiabu.2004.12.005.

Colman, R., & Widom, C. (2004). Childhood abuse and neglect and adult intimate relationships: A prospective study. *Child Abuse & Neglect, 28,* 1133-1151.

Connolly, A., & Woollons, R. (2008). Childhood sexual experience and adult offending: An exploratory comparison of three criminal groups. *Child Abuse Review, 17*(2), 119-132.

Coohey, C. (2010). Gender differences in internalizing problems among sexually abused early adolescents. *Child Abuse & Neglect, 34,* 856-862.

Cortoni, F., & Hanson, R. K. (2005). A review of the recidivism rates of adult female sex offenders. Research report No. R-169. Ottawa, ON: Correctional Service of Canada.

Crossen-Tower, C. (2009). *Understanding child abuse and neglect* (8th ed.). New York: Pearson.

Crowder, A. (1995). *Opening the door: A treatment model for therapy with male survivors of sexual abuse.* NY: Brunner/Mazel.

Doerfler, L., Toscano, P., & Connor, D. (2009). Sex and aggression: The relationship between gender and abuse experience in youngsters referred to residential treatment. *Journal of Child & Family Studies, 18,* 112-122.

Dong, M., Anda, R., Felitti, V., Dube, S., Williamson, D., Thompson, T., . . . & Giles, W. (2004). The interrelatedness of multiple forms of childhood abuse, neglect, and household dysfunction. *Child Abuse & Neglect, 28(7),* 771-784.

Draucker, C. B., & Martsolf, D. (2006). *Counselling survivors of childhood sexual abuse.* London: Nova.

Dube, S., Anda. R., Whitfield, C., Brown, D., Felitti, V., Dong, M., & Giles, W. (2005). consequences of childhood sexual abuse by gender of victim. *American Journal of Preventative Medicine, 28,* 430-438.

Duncan, L. E., & William, L. M. (1998). Gender role socialization and male-on-male vs. female-on-male child sexual abuse. *Sex Roles, 39,* 765-785.

Durham, A. (2003). Young men living through and with child sexual abuse: A practitioner research study. *British Journal of Social Work, 33*(3), 309-323.

Easton, S., Renner, L., & O'Leary, P. (2013). Suicide attempts among men with histories of child sexual abuse: Examining abuse severity, mental health, and masculine norms. *Child Abuse & Neglect, 37,* 380-387.

Feather, J. S., & Ronan, K. R. (2009). Trauma-focused CBT with maltreated children: A clinic-based evaluation of a new treatment manual. *Australian Psychologist, 44,* 174–194. doi:10.1080/00050060903147083.

Finkelhor, D. (2008). *Childhood victimization: Violence, crime, and abuse in the lives of young people.* Oxford, UK: Oxford University Press.

Finkelhor, D., Hammer, H., & Sedlak, A. J. (2008, August). *Sexually assaulted children: National estimates and characteristics.* Bureau of Justice

Statistics, U.S. Department of Justice. Retrieved from http://www.ncjrs.gov/pdffiles1/ojjdp/214383.pdf.

Foa, E. B., Molnar, C., & Cashman, L. (1995). Change in rape narratives during exposure to therapy for Posttraumatic Stress Disorder. *Journal of Traumatic Stress*, *8*, 675-690. doi:10.1002/jts.2490080409.

Foa, E. B., & Rothebaum, B. O. (1998). *Treating the trauma of rape: Cognitive-behavioral therapy for PTSD*. NY: Guilford Press.

Foster, J. M. (2011). *An analysis of trauma narratives: Perceptions of children on the experience of childhood sexual abuse* (Doctoral Dissertation). Retrieved from http://www.worldcat.org/.

Foster, J. M. (2014). Supporting child victims of sexual abuse: Implementation of a trauma narrative family intervention. *The Family Journal, 22*(3) 332-338.

Foster, J. M., & Carson, D. K. (2013). Child sexual abuse in the United States: Perspectives on assessment and intervention. *American Journal of Humanities and Social Sciences, 1*(3), 97-108.

Foster, J. M., & Hagedorn, W. B. (2014a). Through the eyes of the wounded: A narrative analysis of children's sexual abuse experiences and recovery process. *Journal of Child Sexual Abuse, 23*, 538-577.

Foster, J. M., & Hagedorn, W. B. (2014b). A Qualitative Exploration of Fear and Safety with Child Victims of Sexual Abuse. *Journal of Mental Health Counseling. 36*(3), 243-262.

Garnefski N., & Arends, E. (1998). Sexual abuse and adolescent maladjustment: Differences between male and female victims. *Journal of Adolescence, 21*, 99-107.

Gil, E. (2006). *Helping abused and traumatized children: Integrating directive and non-directive approaches*. NY: Guilford Press.

Glasser, M., Kolvin, I., Campbell, D., Glasser, A., Leitch, I., & Farrelly, S. (2001). Cycle of child sexual abuse: Link between being a victim and becoming a perpetrator. *British Journal of Psychiatry, 179*, 482–494.

Gold, S., Lucenko, B., Elhai, J., Swingle, J., & Sellers, A. (1999). A comparison of psychological/psychiatric symptomatology of women and men sexually abused as children. *Child Abuse & Neglect, 23*, 683-692.

Goldfinch, M. (2009). 'Putting humpty together again': Working with parents to help children who have experienced early trauma. *Australian & New Zealand Journal of Family Therapy, 30*(4), 284-299.

Goodman-Brown, T. B., Edelstein, R. S., Goodman, G. S., Jones, D. P. H., & Gordon, D. S. (2003). *Child Abuse & Neglect, 27*, 525-540.

Gore-Felton, C., Koopman, C., Thoresen, C., Arnow, B., Bridges, E., & Spiegel, D. (2000). Psychologists' beliefs and clinical characteristics: Judging the veracity of childhood sexual abuse memories, *Professional Psychology: Research and Practice, 31*(4), 372-377.

Grossman, F. K., Sorsoli, L., & Kia-Keating, M. (2006). A gale force wind: Meaning making by male survivors of childhood sexual abuse. *American Journal of Orthopsychiatry, 76*(4), 434–443.

Hall, K. (2007). Sexual dysfunction and childhood sexual abuse: Gender differences and treatment implications. In S. R. Leiblum (Ed.), *Principles and practices of sex therapy* (pp. 350-378). NY: The Gilford Press.

Hebert, M., Tremblay, C., Parent, N., Daignault, I., & Piche, C. (2006). Correlates of behavioral outcomes in sexually abused children. *Journal of Family Violence, 21,* 287-299.

Holmes, W., & Slap, G. (1998). Sexual abuse of boys: Definition, correlates, sequelae, and management. *Journal of the American Medical Association, 280*(2), 1855-1862.

Homma, Y., Wang, N., Saewyc, E., & Kishor, N. (2012). The relationship between sexual abuse and risky sexual behavior among adolescent boys: A meta-analysis. *Journal of Adolescent Health, 51,* 18-24.

Hopton, J., & Huta, V. (2013). Evaluation of an intervention designed for men who were abused in childhood and are experiencing symptoms of posttraumatic stress disorder. *Psychology of Men & Masculinity, 14*(3), 300-313. doi: 10.1037/a0029705.

Horner, G. (2010). Child sexual abuse: Consequences and implications. *Journal of Pediatric Health Care, 24,* 358-364.

Johnson, C. (2004). Child sexual abuse. *Lancet, 364,* 462-470.

Kaminer, D. (2006). Healing processes in trauma narratives: A review. *South African Journal of Psychology, 36*(3), 481-499.

Kia-Keating, M., Grossman, F., Sorsoli, L., & Epstein, M. (2005). Containing and resisting masculinity: Narratives of renegotiation among resilient male survivors of childhood sexual abuse. *Psychology of Men & Masculinity, 6*(3), 169-185.

Lab, D., Feigenbaum, J., & Silva, P. (2000). Mental health professionals' attitudes and practices towards male childhood sexual abuse. *Child Abuse and Neglect, 24,* 391-409.

Lanktree, C., & Briere, J. (2008). *Integrative treatment of complex trauma for children (ITCT-C): A guide for the treatment of multiply-traumatized children aged eight to twelve years.* Retrieved from http://johnbriere.com/articles.htm.

Lataster, T., van Os, J., Drukker, M., Henquet, C., Feron, F., Gunther, N., & Myin-Germeys, I. (2006). Childhood victimization and developmental expression of non-clinical delusional ideation and hallucinatory experiences: Victimization and non-clinical psychotic 223 experiences. *Social Psychiatry and Psychiatric Epidemiology, 41*(6), 423-428. doi:10.1007/s00127-006-0060-4.

Levant, R. F., Richmond, K., Majors, R. G., Inclan, J. E., Rossello, J. M., Heesacker, M., . . . Sellers, A. (2003). A multicultural investigation of masculinity ideology and alexithymia. *Psychology of Men & Masculinity, 4,* 91–99.

Little, L., & Hamby, S. L. (1999). Gender differences in sexual abuse outcomes and recovery experiences: A survey of therapist-survivors. *Professional Psychology: Research and Practice, 30,* 378–385.

Lobanov-Rostovsky, C. (2014). *Recidivism of juveniles who commit sexual offenses.* (NCJ 247059). Retrieved from http://www.smart.gov/SOMAPI/pdfs/SOMAPI_Full%20Report.pdf.

Loeb, T. B., Williams, J. K., Carmona, J. V., Rivkin, I., Wyatt, G. E., Chin, D. & Asuan-O'Brien, A. (2002). Child sexual abuse: Associations with the sexual functioning of adolescents and adults. *Annual Review of Sex Research, 13,* 307-345.

Long, L. L., Burnett, J. A., & Thomas, R. V. (2006). *Sexuality counseling: An integrative approach.* Upper Saddle River, NJ: Pearson.

Lundqvist, G., Hansson, K., & Svedin, C. G. (2004). The influence of childhood sexual abuse factors on women's health. *Nordic Journal of Psychiatry, 58*(5), 395-401. doi:10.1080/08039480410005963.

McGregor, K., Thomas, D. R., & Read, J. (2006). Therapy for child sexual abuse: Women talk about helpful and unhelpful therapy experiences. *Journal of Child Sexual Abuse, 15*(4), 35-59.

McGuffey, C. (2008). "Saving masculinity": Gender reaffirmation, sexuality, race, and parental responses to male child sexual abuse. *Social Problems, 55*(2), 216-237.

Moody, C. (1999). Male child sexual abuse. *Journal of Pediatric Health Care, 13*(3), 112-119.

Murray, J. B. (2000). Psychological profile of pedophiles and child molesters. *The Journal of Psychology, 134*(2), 211-224. doi:10.1080/00223980 009600863.

Nilsson, D., Gustafsson, P. E., & Svedin, C. G. (2012). Polytraumatization and trauma symptoms in adolescent boys and girls: Interpersonal and noninterpersonal events and moderating effects of adverse family circumstances. *Journal of Interpersonal Violence, 27*(13), 2645-2664. http://dx.doi.org/10.1177/0886260512436386.

Nisbet-Wallis, D. A. (2002). Reduction in trauma symptoms following group therapy. *Australian and New Zealand Journal of Psychiatry, 36*(1), 67-74. doi:10.1046/j.1440-1614.2002.00980.

Oz, S. (2005). The "wall of fear": The bridge between the traumatic event and trauma resolution therapy for childhood sexual abuse survivors. *Journal of Child Sexual Abuse, 14*(3), 23-47.

Parker, A., Fourt, A., Langmuir, J. I., Dalton, E. J., & Classen, C. C. (2007). The experience of trauma recovery: A qualitative study of participants in the women recovering from abuse program (WRAP). *Journal of Child Sexual Abuse, 16*(2), 55-77. doi:10.1300/J070v16n02_04.

Pereda, N., Guilera, G., Forns, M., & Gomez-Benito, J. (2009). The prevalence of child sexual abuse in community and student samples: A meta-analysis. *Clinical Psychology Review, 29,* 328-338.

Perez-Fuentes, G., Olfson, M., Villegas, L., Morcillo, C., Wang, S., & Blanco, C. (2013). Prevalence and correlates of child sexual abuse: A national study. *Comprehensive Psychiatry, 54,* 16-27.

Przybylski, R. (2014). *Adult Sex Offender Recidivism.* (NCJ 247059). Retrieved from http://www.smart.gov/SOMAPI/pdfs/SOMAPI_Full%20Report.

Ray, S. (2001). Male survivors' perspectives of incest/sexual abuse. *Perspectives in Psychiatric Care, 37,* 49-59.

Read, J., Goodman, L., Morrison, A. P., Ross, C. A., & Aderhold, V. (2004). Childhood trauma, loss and stress. In J. Read, L. Mosher, & R. Bentall (Eds.), *Model of madness: Psychological, social and biological approaches to schizophrenia* (pp. 223–252). Hove, England: Brunner-Routledge.

Rencken, R. H. (2000). *Brief and extended interventions in sexual abuse.* Alexandria, VA: American Counseling Association.

Romano, E., & De Luca, R. V. (2001) Male sexual abuse: A review of effects, abuse characteristics, and links with later psychological functioning. *Aggression and Violent Behavior, 6*(1), 55-78.

Sandler, J. C., & Freeman, N. J. (2009). Female sex offender recidivism: A large-scale empirical analysis. *Sexual Abuse: A Journal of Research and Treatment, 21,* 455–473.

Sandoval, J., Scott, A. N., & Padilla, I. (2009). Crisis counseling: An overview. *Psychology in the Schools, 46*(3), 246-256.

Schauer, E., Neuner, F., Elbert, T., Ertl, V., Onyut, L. P., Odenwald, M., & Schauer, M. (2004). Narrative exposure therapy in children: A case study. *Intervention, 2*(1), 18-32.

Schraufnagel, T., Davis, K., George, W., & Norris, J. (2010). Childhood sexual abuse in males and subsequent risky sexual behavior: A potential alcohol-use pathway. *Child Abuse & Neglect, 34,* 369-378.

Sheinberg, M., & True, F. (2008). Treating family relational trauma: A recursive process using a decision dialogue. *Family Process, 47,* 173–195. doi:10.1111/j.1545-5300.2008.00247.x.

Silverman, W. K., Ortiz, C. D., Viswesvaran, C., Burns, B. J., Kolko, D. J., Putnam, F. W., & Amaya-Jackson, L. (2008). Evidence-based psychosocial treatments for children and adolescents exposed to traumatic events. *Journal of Clinical Child and Adolescent Psychology, 37,* 156–183. doi:10.1080/15374410701818293.

Snyder, H. (2000, July). *Sexual assault of young children as reported to law enforcement: Victim, incident and offender characteristics.* Bureau of Justice Statistics, U.S. Department of Justice. Retrieved from http://bjs.ojp.usdoj.gov/content/pub/pdf/saycrle.pdf.

Sonnby, K., Aslund, C., Leppert, J., & Nilsson, K. (2011). Symptoms of ADHD and depression in a large adolescent population: Co-occurring symptoms and associations to experiences of sexual abuse. *Nordic Journal of Psychiatry, 65,* 315-322.

Sorsoli, L., Kia-Keating, M., & Grossman, F. (2008). I keep that hush-hush: Male survivors of sexual abuse and the challenges of disclosure. *Journal of Counseling Psychology, 55*(3), 333-345.

Spiegel, J. (2003). *The sexual abuse of males: The SAM model of theory and practice.* NY: Brunner-Routledge.

Tomlinson, P. (2008). Assessing the needs of traumatized children to improve outcomes. *Journal of Social Work Practice, 22*(3), 359-374.

Tremblay, C., Hebert, M., & Piche, C. (1999). Coping strategies and social support as mediators of consequences in child sexual abuse victims, *Child Abuse and Neglect, 23*(9), 929-945.

Ullman, S. E. (2003). Social reactions to child sexual abuse disclosures: A critical review. *Journal of Child Sexual Abuse, 12,* 89-121. doi:10.1300/J070v12n01_05.

U.S. Department of Health and Human Services, Administration for Children and Families, Administration on Children, Youth and Families, Children's Bureau. (2013). *Child Maltreatment 2012.* Available from http://www.acf.

hhs.gov/programs/cb/research-data-technology/statistics-research/child-maltreatment.

Valente, S. (2005). Sexual abuse of boys. *Journal of Child and Adolescent Psychiatric Nursing, 18*(1), 10-16.

Ward, T., & Beech, A. (2005). An integrated theory of sexual offending. *Aggression and Violent Behavior: A Review Journal, 11*, 44-63.

Watts, S., & McNulty, T. (2013). Childhood abuse and criminal behavior: Testing a general strain theory model. *Journal of Interpersonal Violence, 28*(15), 3023-3040.

Webster, R. E. (2001). Symptoms and long-term outcomes for children who have been sexually assaulted. *Psychology in the Schools, 38(6),* 533-549.

Welfare, A. (2008). How qualitative research can inform clinical interventions in families recovering from sibling sexual abuse. *Australian and New Zealand Journal of Family Therapy, 29*(3), 139-147. doi:10.1375/anft. 29.3.139.

West, D. (1998). Boys and sexual abuse: An English opinion. *Archives of Sexual Behavior, 27*(6), 539-559.

Wilhite, M. L. (2015). The silent victims of childhood sexual abuse: Treatment considerations for male survivors. (Doctoral dissertation). Retrieved from ProQuest Dissertations and Theses database. (UMI No. 3701240)

INDEX

A

age at the onset, 104
alternative, vii, viii, 2, 4, 18, 48, 58
Anger, 5
ashamed, 5, 103, 107
asymptomatic, 92, 110

B

beliefs, 8, 12, 13, 35, 36, 50, 57, 58, 63, 66,
    69, 70, 72, 73, 74, 104, 105, 107, 112,
    113, 119, 124
betrayal, 7, 12, 30, 96, 108, 120
biases, 56, 114
blame, 3, 5, 6, 13, 15, 29, 34, 55, 74, 93

C

Caregivers, 1, 114
Centers for Disease Control and Prevention,
    vii, 1, 2, 19, 121
Child on child sexual abuse, 106
childhood sexual abuse, vii, ix, 22, 80, 85,
    89, 90, 91, 92, 93, 95, 97, 98, 99, 102,
    120, 122, 123, 124, 125, 126, 127, 128
concealment, 81, 103
confusion, 6, 56, 95, 96, 108, 113, 117
conviction rates, 6, 28

Coping Skills, 13
coping strategies, vii, 23, 85, 96, 117, 119,
    127
covert, 90, 102
cross-examinations, 110

D

definition, 27, 31, 90, 91, 92, 102, 103, 124
dependence, 7, 108
Disbelief, 5
disclosure, vii, viii, x, 1, 2, 3, 4, 5, 8, 10, 12,
    16, 20, 28, 34, 46, 49, 51, 54, 55, 60, 68,
    70, 80, 81, 82, 101, 103, 107, 108, 109,
    110, 116, 119, 127
dropout, 19, 115, 121
dysfunctional cognitions, 112

E

early intervention, viii, 26, 34, 110, 115
egocentrism, 108
empathy, 117
environmental commonalities, 104
externalizing behaviors, 110, 111

F

family session, 16, 18, 115

fear(s), 8, 12, 14, 15, 20, 21, 22, 29, 34, 53,
    54, 55, 61, 63, 65, 103, 107, 108, 109,
    112, 113, 114, 115, 123, 126
female perpetrators, 106, 114
female-on-male sexual assault, 109
financial, 4, 7, 8, 9, 13, 51, 69, 77, 102
Financial Challenges, 8
Forgiveness, 14
Four Phase Model, 116
Future, 18, 39, 98, 118

G

gender norms, 107, 109
gender role expectations, 107
generalizability, x, 101, 102, 104
Group Counseling, 4
Group Curriculum, 12
Group Dynamics, 10
group format, 4, 9, 10, 12, 18, 118
group size, 11
guilt, 3, 5, 6, 13, 29, 34, 63, 93, 96, 108,
    112, 113

H

healing, x, 4, 9, 10, 15, 16, 18, 21, 72, 76,
    101, 103, 110, 111, 115, 118, 119, 120,
    124
Healing Journey, 118
homosexual, 103, 107, 108, 113, 114
homosexuality, 52, 55, 70, 109, 114

I

identity, 85, 96, 108, 116, 118
incidents, 102, 106
income, 8
Initial Reactions, 12
instability, 7, 9
internalizing behaviors, 111
invisibility, 102

J

juvenile offenders, 106

L

Leadership, 10
Long-Term, 111
loss, 4, 5, 7, 8, 114, 126

M

masculine identity, 107
masculinity, 103, 109, 113, 117, 119, 120,
    124, 125

N

narratives, 5, 15, 16, 59, 107, 110, 123, 124
negative outcomes, viii, 1, 2, 4, 111, 115
Nonoffending Parents, 1, 114

O

obstacles, 65, 107, 109, 119
Open Format, 10
opportunists, 106
overt, 90, 102

P

parallel interventions, vii, viii, 2, 4, 18
parental factors, 105
parental incest, 16, 17
parental support, 3
Parenting, 14, 37, 79
penetration, 3, 30, 95, 102, 106, 111
Personal Reactions, 5
pleasure, 28, 108, 113
Post-Abuse Life, 13
Prevalence, 99, 102, 103, 126
proactive parenting, 14

protective parent, 3
psychoeducation, 12, 39
psycho-education, 114
Psychoeducation, 12
psychological distress, 110
psychological impact, vii, ix, 85, 89, 90

R

rapport, 58, 59, 60, 113
recidivism, 106, 122, 125, 126
recollections, x, 101, 102
recovery, 21, 103, 110, 123, 125, 126
referrals, 10, 11
regret, 8
Relational Changes, 7
religious, vii, ix, 2, 8, 45, 46, 47, 48, 49, 50,
    51, 52, 55, 57, 58, 60, 63, 64, 65, 66, 67,
    68, 69, 70, 72, 73, 74, 75, 76, 77, 79, 82,
    85
relocation, 9
resiliency, 118, 119
responsibility, 27, 64, 69, 70, 72, 107, 108,
    113
reunification, 17
re-victimized, 112

S

sadistic, 105
sadness, 3, 5, 7, 8, 13, 114
SAM Model, 116
screening procedures, 11
self-identification, 104
sexual functioning, 117, 125
sexual orientation, 105, 113
sibling sexual abuse, 3, 16, 17, 23, 106, 128

stigma, 28, 35, 107, 114, 119, 120
stranger initiated sexual abuse, 2
suicide, 31, 40, 82, 111, 122
support, viii, 3, 4, 7, 8, 9, 10, 11, 14, 15, 16,
    17, 21, 23, 26, 33, 37, 38, 51, 57, 64, 69,
    72, 74, 76, 77, 78, 86, 96, 110, 111, 114,
    118, 119, 120, 127
symptomology, vii, viii, 1, 4, 95, 115
symptoms, viii, x, 1, 2, 4, 5, 6, 12, 15, 18,
    19, 29, 32, 35, 42, 89, 90, 91, 92, 93, 94,
    95, 97, 98, 110, 111, 112, 115, 117, 119,
    124, 125, 126, 127, 128

T

terminate, 19
threats, 108
training, 10, 37, 76, 77, 83, 85, 87, 120
transitions, 4, 9
Trauma Focused Cognitive Behavioral
    Therapy, 15, 112
trauma narrative intervention, 115
trust, 2, 3, 27, 28, 32, 60, 63, 73, 75, 76, 96,
    113, 117

U

universality, 9
unprocessed trauma, 115
USA, 1, 101

V

violent, 22, 31, 63, 93, 106, 126, 128